Praise for *Happiness is Down Syndrome*

"Misty Coy Snyder has created a beautiful blend of honesty, compassion, and real-life guidance for families navigating a Down syndrome diagnosis. With both tenderness and truth, she creates space for every emotion—grief, hope, fear, and joy—while gently reminding readers that they are not alone on this journey. This book is not just a resource, but a companion for parents at every stage, offering encouragement, perspective, and a powerful vision of what is possible."

—Camille Joy,
advocate for families of children
with special needs

"Misty has written a must read for the parent/guardian of a child with Down syndrome! I wish that I could have read this fantastic book 26 years ago. Absolutely tremendous!"

—Patti Nikic,
mother of Chris Nikic, a 26-year-old triathlete with
Down syndrome who set four Guinness World Records,
is an Adidas-sponsored athlete, a Special Olympics
World Ambassador, recipient of the Laureus Best Sporting
Moment of the Year award, and motivational speaker

"Misty Snyder is the embodiment of what true community looks like. She is a bright light for families navigating a Down syndrome diagnosis. Through her platform and her voice, she has created a space where families feel seen, supported, and deeply understood.

Happiness is Down Syndrome is a reflection of that same heart. It is real, raw, and deeply informative, offering an honest glimpse into the lived experience of raising a child with Down syndrome. Misty captures both the reality alongside the extraordinary joys with authenticity and grace, reminding readers that what may first feel uncertain can become one of life's greatest blessings.

(*continued*)

This book is not only a powerful resource, but a source of hope, encouragement, and connection for any family on this journey."

—Lauren Costabile,
Founder and Executive Director of
Hearts of Joy International

"When my daughter Nova was born with Down syndrome, another mother in my life helped me see beyond the diagnosis and into the extraordinary possibilities, path, and future that lay ahead. When Misty later became a mother to her own son with Down syndrome, she reached out to me to participate in a beautiful project that helped shape her journey and share it with others. It addressed something that had felt deeply lacking in my own experience as a new parent.

One of the common threads in conversations among parents of children with Down syndrome is the need for more resources that are practical, hopeful, balanced, and rooted in real lived experience. I have watched Misty transform her love for her son and her family into a powerful force for advocacy, education, and hope—not only within our community, but internationally.

As her friend, I stand in awe of all she has accomplished and the countless families she has already impacted. This book is the resource every parent deserves at the start of their journey. Honest, informative, and deeply compassionate, it offers the reassurance that raising a child with Down syndrome is not something to fear, but one of life's most meaningful and unexpected gifts."

—Haven Burton,
Broadway performer, voice actor,
and mother of three

"As a friend and fellow parent advocate on this journey, I know the heart and honesty Misty brings to this work. This book is real, lived, and deeply needed. It's something families will actually use, not just read."

—Tonye Faloughi-Ekezie,
CEO of Simone's Oasis Foundation

"Misty is uniquely qualified to speak on this subject because she writes from a place no textbook or theory can replicate—real life. As a mother raising a child with Down syndrome, she brings first-hand insight into the joys, challenges, growth, and unexpected blessings that come with the journey. Her voice carries credibility because it is rooted in daily experiences, deep love, and a genuine commitment to reshaping how the world views Down syndrome."

—Ashley Piazza Odom,
President/Executive Director of
FRIENDS Down Syndrome Special Needs

"As a fellow mom raising a child with Down syndrome, so much of this book felt deeply personal to me, making me wish I had it in those early days. Misty has captured the fear, grief, beauty, wonder, and unexpected joy of this great journey while also being honest and compassionate."

—Rachael Lampa,
award winning vocal artist in Contemporary
Christian Music and mother of a child with Down syndrome

"I really enjoy reading books about new mothers who navigate through the uncharted territory of receiving the diagnosis of Down syndrome and finding community. The initial fears Misty had about her son reminds me of those my own mom had when I was born with Down syndrome. I liked how Dr. Brian Skotko was mentioned in the excerpt because he has a sister with Down syndrome and that he is working tirelessly on co-occurring health conditions that people with Down syndrome may develop as they age. I also love the new mother's genetic counselor too. I like how the genetic counselor didn't make low expectations or paint a grim future about her son's future abilities like the doctors did with my mom. We need more genetic counselors as well as doctors who are compassionate and empathetic towards new pregnant mothers going through tough times. Reading this book has solidified my resolve to help new mothers find community and to educate doctors about the urgent need for them to look beyond the Down syndrome diagnosis

(*continued*)

of people with Down syndrome and stop perpetuating low expectations, myths, misconceptions, and stereotypes. I would definitely recommend this book to any new mother who is pregnant with a baby that may be born with Down syndrome! I would like to see new mothers fostering friendships and bonding together in order to find community as a result of reading this book."

—Charlotte Woodward,
Programs Associate at National Down Syndrome Society

"Through her storytelling, Misty offers a perspective that feels both honest and connected to the lived experiences of our community. Her voice uplifts and reminds the world of what we know to be true every day. NDSS welcomes thoughtful work like this that adds to the broader conversations, and I am grateful to stand alongside this fellow mom in advocacy."

—Kandi Pickard,
CEO, National Down Syndrome Society

"With heartfelt vulnerability and hope, Misty Coy Snyder has created a powerful resource for families navigating a Down syndrome diagnosis. Her honesty, advocacy, and lived experience will make countless parents feel seen, encouraged, and deeply supported."

—Amy Amaradio,
Founder and President, Dear Mom

Happiness is Down Syndrome

Happiness is Down Syndrome

STRATEGIES AND SUPPORT FOR PARENTS AT EVERY STAGE

MISTY COY SNYDER

JB JOSSEY-BASS™
A Wiley Brand

Published by John Wiley & Sons, Inc., Hoboken, New Jersey.

For general information on our other products and services or for technical support, please contact our Customer Care Department within the United States at (800) 762-2974, outside the United States at (317) 572-3993 or fax (317) 572-4002.

Wiley also publishes its books in a variety of electronic formats. Some content that appears in print may not be available in electronic formats. For more information about Wiley products, visit our website at www.wiley.com.

Library of Congress Cataloging-in-Publication Data is Available:

ISBN 9781394352531 (Paperback)
ISBN 9781394352548 (ePub)
ISBN 9781394352555 (ePDF)

Cover Design: Paul McCarthy
Illustrations: Tiffany Fuller

SKY10161667_070726

To Braden, Clay, and Jed: you made this labor of love possible. I love you.

Contents

Foreword

There are moments in life when experience alone is not enough—when families need both truth and tenderness, both expertise and empathy. Over the years, through my work in the Down syndrome community, I have walked alongside thousands of parents, caregivers, and advocates who find themselves suddenly standing in unfamiliar territory. Regardless of where their journey begins—a prenatal diagnosis, a birth diagnosis, or a growing awareness of what lies ahead—one common thread remains: the deep desire to understand, to feel less alone, and to believe that hope is still possible.

It is in that sacred space that this book belongs.

I have known Misty Coy Snyder not only as a fellow professional in the Down syndrome space, but as a friend. I have witnessed firsthand the way she shows up—with honesty, humility, and an unwavering commitment to families who are navigating fear, grief, and uncertainty. Misty does not speak from a place of theory or assumption. She speaks from lived experience, from countless conversations with parents around the world, and from a heart that has been shaped and softened by love.

What makes this book so powerful is not that it avoids the hard parts—it doesn't. Misty names the fear many parents feel but are afraid to say out loud. She acknowledges the grief that can exist alongside joy. She gives language to emotions that so often live in silence. And yet, she does all of this without despair. Instead, she gently guides the reader toward connection, understanding, and hope—not as a destination to rush toward, but as something that grows one step at a time.

As someone who works daily in guiding families through the complexities of raising a loved one who has a disability, I can say with confidence that this book fills a critical gap. Too often, families are given information without compassion or encouragement without honesty. Misty offers both. Through her storytelling, research, and the voices of others in the community, she creates a space where readers can breathe, learn, and begin again—without pressure to "fix" their feelings or arrive at acceptance on anyone else's timeline.

These pages are written with care and compassion, not as a formula or explanation for life's challenges, but as a steady companion—reminding us that even when the road is uncertain, we are not walking it alone. This is not a book that tells you what to feel. It is a book that walks with you while you feel it.

If you are holding this book in your hands feeling overwhelmed, unsure, or afraid of what lies ahead, know this: you are not behind, you are not broken, and you are not alone. Misty's words will meet you exactly where you are—and gently remind you that there is beauty, connection, and purpose waiting to unfold. This book also invites you to catch the vision of what might be for your loved one with Down syndrome, to see their unique gifts, and to help unlock the potential for them to sing the song they are meant to sing, in ways that will inspire and uplift both them and you.

It is an honor to introduce this work, and an even greater honor to call Misty Coy Snyder a colleague, a partner in advocacy, and a friend.

With deep respect and gratitude,
Brady Murray, CFP®, ChSNC
Founder, CaringTide
Founder, RODS Heroes

Introduction

"I wish for a world that views disability, mental or physical, not as a hindrance but as unique attributes that can be seen as powerful assets if given the right opportunities."

—Oliver Sacks

My luck had run out.

Eleven years ago I was rushing to an audition in New York City on a blustery November day. My subway halted underground, for no apparent reason, and when I finally arrived at my stop, I was flustered and worried I was going to be late. Holiday bustle was in the air, above ground, and thousands of people swarmed the streets of midtown Manhattan like ants to a giant breadcrumb. As I rushed toward my destination, I began to feel a glimmer of hope that I might make it on time when I saw something that stopped me in my tracks.

There, in front of a building well known to aspiring actors, a group of tourists with disabilities stood directly in front of the entrance, pointing up. One young man, with almond-shaped eyes and speech that was difficult to decipher, smiled and spoke to me as I tried to maneuver myself around him. I shot him a grin and said, "Excuse me" with an irritable tone I'd unsuccessfully tried to mask. He was undeterred by my reaction and said, "Look at the Empire State Building" with excitement emanating from his voice. I glanced in the direction he pointed and saw the tall skyscraper I'd admired as a tourist, once upon a time. I flashed a quick smile again and said, "Yeah, it's pretty cool" as I pushed and shoved my way through the revolving door.

I ran into the elevator and had **21** flights to catch my breath and reflect on what had just transpired. I felt an odd twinge of warmth in my heart after encountering the group outside but it was overshadowed by my annoyance. I couldn't believe my **luck**. I was definitely going to be late! What were the odds of a subway delay AND an **extra** delay from a group like that? The faces of disability were as foreign to me as Greek or Latin and my encounter felt uncomfortable and untimely. At this moment in time, in my early thirties, I certainly didn't view the disability in that man as a "powerful asset," the way Oliver Sacks describes in the quote above. Quite the opposite. I would have preferred to avoid him altogether.

Aside from that day in New York City, encounters like this had been rare for me. Virtually nil.

Eleven years ago, that's exactly how I liked it. Equal, of course, but very separate from anyone who didn't fit my box of conformity. My unvoiced and mostly unidentified expectations of perfection and "normalcy" were comfortable and cushy for me. And though I didn't get the role I auditioned for that day in NYC, it was a disappointment I could accept and live with. My tolerance level was nowhere near as high for those with disabilities.

Today, it's hard to identify with the actress pounding the concrete jungle so many years ago. Presently, I sit in a coffee shop compiling a book of stories, resources, organizations, and encouragement for a community I once actively dodged. A community I now belong to. One that is often referred to as "The Lucky Few" (a phrase Heather Avis coined in 2015 that sparked a movement and went on to be the title of her first book in 2017, *The* ***Lucky*** *Few: Finding God's Best in the Most Unlikely Places*). It's a tough pill to swallow and even tougher to admit in print, for the world to see. But it's necessary to come to terms with this prior version of myself, and doing so may pave a way for connection with hundreds of thousands who may feel the same way. Even if they don't care to admit it.

Maybe that's you?

Maybe you're afraid. Angry. Confused. Shaking your fists.

Maybe you don't relate to any of those descriptions, but you feel alone on the journey.

Maybe you're a friend or family member who wants to know more so they can serve from a place of genuine authenticity and understanding. So let's begin by saying the words I've skipped over, up to now—*Down syndrome*.

Seeing those words in black and white may evoke a variety of emotions but the most frequent one I hear about is: *fear*.

I spent most of my life afraid based on what I THOUGHT I knew about Down syndrome.

I THOUGHT my son's extra chromosome was caused by my maternal age. I felt immediate regret about having a baby past the age of 35. Perhaps you are feeling a similar kind of way or, if you are younger, you might be wondering how this diagnosis could have found *you*. But as you immerse yourself in the Down syndrome community you will come to see, dear reader, that having a baby with Down syndrome is not exclusive to advanced maternity. Down syndrome occurs randomly across all nationalities, ethnicities, socioeconomic groups, ages, and backgrounds. There was nothing and is nothing to feel regret about because A) nothing I did caused it and B) there is nothing "wrong" with having a child with Down syndrome.

I THOUGHT having a son with Down syndrome would narrow my life's trajectory. I believed our family would be isolated and left in the dust. I presumed my world would become smaller. I envisioned my dreams fading into oblivion and pictured stark, depressing monotony. But there is nothing sparse or thin about this life I am living alongside my son with Down syndrome and our family. In fact, our lives have burst wide open with mindset shifts and colors of every hue through exposure to the most beautiful and diverse community.

I THOUGHT people outside the Down syndrome community would run from us. Instead people flock to my son Jed and the platform I've grown, Happiness is Down Syndrome, *because* of the magic he and other individuals with an extra chromosome have sprinkled into the lives of those around them. My professional work is now directly linked to my son with Down syndrome, and the impact is trickling down to all who encounter him. Just today at the park, a little boy from his school shouted across the field, "Jed! It's Jed!" and proceeded to follow him around and play with him on all the equipment. That kind of genuine connection and love cannot be manufactured.

I THOUGHT having a son with a disability would negatively impact my typically developing, firstborn son. I worried that he would feel ashamed or burdened by having a brother with Down syndrome and I assumed our lives would be insanely dark and grim. I feared he would resent his little brother and us, his parents.

Yet, only five years into Jed's life, I continue to gratefully bear witness to the most beautiful bond. It's so very different from the nightmare I conjured up in my mind before I woke.

It's clear this journey is not cut and dried, nor a one-size-fits-all prescription. However, so much of what I THOUGHT to be true, has proved to be untrue and I've heard and read similar sentiments from those in our community time and time again. Conversely, many bountiful blessings I never would have expected have burst onto the scene. I'm not the only one who came to the table with incorrect perceptions and ideas about Down syndrome. Our society has been conditioned for decades (*centuries*, most likely) to think that neurodivergence is something to be feared and avoided at all costs. My reaction to the tourists in NYC only further cements that.

What I Am and Am Not

As you begin reading, I confess that **I AM NOT:**

- A doctor
- A therapist
- A lawyer
- A financial planner
- A scientist
- A counselor

I am proud to say that **I AM:**

- A mother of a child with Down syndrome
- An advocate
- A passionate leader in the Down syndrome community
- A connector

I have spent countless hours of my life researching, advocating, and reaching out to others who have gone before me in the Down syndrome community. I've made myself available to newly diagnosed families through my platform Happiness is Down Syndrome and, as a result, I've connected with families and individuals from more than 36 countries throughout the globe, some of whom I met in person when I spoke at the United Nations this past March. This community is my heartbeat. My life's mission.

As you embark on this journey, whether as a parent, grandparent, family member, friend, or ally, I encourage you to:

- Look further into the history of Down syndrome. Some of it will be painful to uncover but we can't progress and forge new victories without knowing the roots of the bias and ableism that still exist.
- Take a look at the scientific work that has been done in recent years and the studies that shed light on the intricacies and unique characteristics of our loved ones.
- Enlighten your mind by exploring the invaluable work (past, present, and moving into the future) of therapists, doctors, and specialists who have worked and continue to trudge ahead tirelessly to accurately portray the trials and triumphs of this road.
- Recognize that there is no be-all and end-all when it comes to treatments, therapies, or learning methods for individuals with Down syndrome. Just as with any person, no two are the same and growth and development are as unique and varied as grains of sand on the beach.

What This Book Is

To illustrate the last point, I have to share a story about learning the hard way.

When my son was almost three years old, I posted a video online of him hiking on a trail in the woods with our whole family. He navigated over roots, bumps, and rocks quite well on his own and didn't need my help. A friend of mine in the Down syndrome community told me that her daughter was not yet able to do that on her own and how my video stirred up some difficult emotions in her. She felt a deep longing for her daughter to be able to navigate confidently through rough terrain.

Ironically, I had just watched a video of *her* daughter singing the full alphabet on her social media page and was discouraged that Jed was not yet close to the same level. When we realized we were both struggling with a similar comparison trap, we laughed and cried together. It was healing to know that, though our challenges were different, we were united by a similar longing—for our children to grow, soar, and experience all the world has to offer. We also acknowledged that comparing was a waste of our energy. Instead, we could rejoice in the victories of both of our unique and beautiful children.

When we agonize about our children not meeting a milestone at the same time as their typical peers or even their peers with Down syndrome, we are robbing them of their individuality and their freedom to explore and learn on their own timeline. We are also putting undue pressure on ourselves to meet some unspoken expectation or cross an invisible finish line or prerequisite. Isn't it better for each parent to set out to do *their* personal best with the child and the tools *they've* been given. Comparison is the thief of joy.

As you comb through the pages of this book, please keep in mind that the landscape surrounding Down syndrome is bound to change, adapt, and shift as the years go by. Important research continues to be conducted and the barometer for what is possible for those with Down syndrome continues to be raised. Brian Stotko, a Board-certified medical geneticist who has a sister with Down syndrome and has dedicated his professional energies toward children with cognitive and developmental disabilities, shared the following on one of his platforms:

> "The way I practice medicine today is really different to how I practiced medicine five years ago or even ten years ago for people with Down syndrome. And that's not because the chromosome has changed or the genetics have changed, it's because we have better information thanks to research that has been going on for the past decade or so for people with Down syndrome. When we see people with Down syndrome in clinic, there are still many unanswered questions that we have on how best to practice medicine and it really is the research that is allowing us to answer those questions. An investment in people with Down syndrome is also an investment in all of us. Did you know that people with Down syndrome have three copies of the gene that encodes for plaques

> that leads to Alzheimer's Disease? So people with Down syndrome might very well have the key to unlock the mystery of Alzheimer's for the rest of us. So as we invest in research about Down syndrome, we are also investing in research for all of us. As we go forward it is my urgent hope that research for people with Down syndrome remains strong and doesn't get cut or scaled back. People with Down syndrome are living healthier, happier, longer lives but we should continue to create more momentum and push that forward and we can only do that when we have research behind us."[1]

In the coming chapters, please consider me a guide or a friend holding your hand through the ups and downs of the "what ifs" that you may be holding today or the ones that may spring up as you read. If overwhelm or fear start to rear their ugly little heads, set the book down for a few minutes and go for a walk. If there is a chapter that feels daunting, skip to another chapter (Chapter 14 is guaranteed to fill you with hope and possibility).

I recommend grace and care for yourself as you read because I remember what it was like in the early days. I was desperate to find answers to nuanced questions in the pages of each book I read and I often felt more questions rise to the surface the more I learned. It can be overwhelming in the beginning and all of us walking that path have felt that surge of, "I don't know what I'm doing," course through our veins. *I still feel that today, sometimes!* It's my deepest desire, however, that your natural concerns will be far surpassed by deep love, respect, and devotion for your loved one with Down syndrome. I want YOU to feel encouraged and empowered to do the best you can with what you've been given.

Let's Start at the Very Beginning

In an effort to connect in a deeper way with those who may be brand new to this journey, I sat down for lunch with a mother who is pregnant with a baby who will most likely have Down syndrome. She resides in New Jersey with her husband, Tanner, and son, Oliver, and she is passionate about women's empowerment and holistic well-being. We were just connected a few weeks ago and she was gracious enough to share some of her spontaneous thoughts during our first lunch together. Here are glimpses of our transcribed voice note recording:

Misty: **Will you share a bit about who you are and what stage of this journey you are in?**

Kaitlin: My name's Kaitlin and I'm 36 weeks pregnant today with my second child—a baby girl. I have an almost three-year-old, Oliver, who's a joy and my baby girl is very highly likely to have Down syndrome. So that's where we are. Today is my first day of maternity leave, so we are getting within a few weeks of meeting her.

Misty: **What were some questions that kept you up at night, early on? Questions that you feel might be relatable to another caregiver in the Down syndrome community right now**?

Kaitlin: Well, the first thing I read online was that 50% of children with Down syndrome have a congenital heart defect. So my biggest concern was my baby's heart. The second was about disability services. I'm not a special education teacher or an OT or PT. So I was really worried about how to get access to that. Can we afford that? Will it be enough for my child? Am I going to have to quit my job and go figure out how to be a PT and OT and all these new things, full time so I can make sure she has what she needs?

Misty: **What would you say to somebody who just heard the news this week?**

Kaitlin: Be kind to yourself. Bringing a child into the world is not easy, but you never expect to be the 1 in 700 babies born with Down syndrome in the U.S., right? It's such a small percentage, so you never think you're gonna be the one. There is a lot of shame that comes with the news because you can feel like, "Do I love my baby? OF COURSE I love my baby, but I don't know how to feel about this!" So just be kind to yourself. You do not have to share the news with everybody. You are entitled to privacy. Share what you want, when you want. Or don't.

Misty: **What are you feeling? What are your primary emotions right now being so close to meeting her?**

Kaitlin: So much anticipation. There were a lot of weeks we didn't know if we would get to this spot because we had heard some scary statistics from doctors. I was just worried she would come early and be in the NICU for months and years. I can't wait to meet her and see her cute little face. We can find out what she needs in the weeks and months and years to come. It's going to be a HUGE celebration when we finally get to meet her.

Misty: **I'm so excited for you, Kaitlin.**

Kaitlin: Mm hmm. I'm so excited.

And to YOU, dear reader, I'm excited for you. No matter where you are in the process and what role you're playing along this path. You can do this. One step at a time.

A Little Extra

If you're reading this with an overwhelming sense of fear to even begin to crack open the pages of this book, I assure you that I have walked where you walk. You WILL make it through. You've come this far! If you experience feelings of worry, sadness, anxiety, excitement, anticipation, or anything else while reading, please know that every single emotion is ok and welcome here!

Your feelings are real and normal and subject to change from day to day or even hour to hour. Each person walking this path has permission to feel all the emotions that rise up as you process this news. It does not make you less of a loving caregiver to have these emotions. And among family members, there may be different reactions to the news. That is also ok. Acceptance is key for yourself and others, alongside you.

The stories, resources, and facts in these pages are meant to encourage and help you feel less alone on the journey. How can I guarantee that? Because I've walked this path for a few years. I have experienced the highs and lows, firsthand. Some people in this book have been around much longer than I, and have a great deal of wisdom to share. Collecting, reading, and compiling these personal accounts has been like a love letter to a part of myself that was once afraid to embark into these uncharted waters. The key to kicking out fear is exposure, knowledge, connection, and hope. You will find all of that in the pages of this book; I'm confident of it!

Happiness is Down Syndrome

CHAPTER 1

The Call That Changed My Life

"For happiness is anyone and anything at all that's loved by you."

—From the musical, You're a Good Man, Charlie Brown

Everything around me froze.

The voice on the other end of the phone sounded like a muffled, underwater siren handing me a death sentence. Cold. Removed. Terrifyingly robotic and sterile.

"The fetus has a 9/10 chance of having Trisomy 21."

"What do you mean," I said, "Like, Down syndrome?"

"Yes. I'm sorry."

Just an hour before I had been driving home from an event. It was March 6, 2020, and although it was still very cold, I noticed that the black, bare trees whizzing past seemed to have a bit more life in them. Maybe even a few buds of spring? I could have been imagining it, of course, because I was wearing rose colored glasses at the time. I was pregnant with my second child and, aside from the pure exhaustion of the first trimester, I was feeling tremendously hope-filled. I was excited and grateful for this rainbow baby growing inside of me. Just a few months before, I'd experienced a miscarriage and the physical, emotional, and spiritual pain had been devastating.

But this time . . .

THIS pregnancy was destined to be different! I could feel it in every fiber of my being. I'd recently heard the heartbeat and surpassed the week where my other pregnancy abruptly halted. As I drove home, there was a brightness to the brisk, late winter day. I'll never forget that feeling of calm, cool contentment before the impending storm.

As soon as I got home, I threw off my winter boots, changed into my pajamas, and wriggled beneath the covers for a quick nap while my two-year-old son slept soundly in his crib. I began to drift off to dreamland when, out of nowhere, I bolted up and looked at my phone, which had been on silent mode. The letters "OB" flashed across my screen, and I immediately swiped to answer. This was it—the moment I would find out the sex of the baby! The prenatal testing I had done was for *this call.* So I could prepare and plan for the colors of the nursery.

In a flash my mind went from pink or blue to black and white. White noise. Stark silence in between awkward utterances of a doctor who apologized with every word, spoken and unspoken.

"Down syndrome" reverberated between my ears over and over again like an echo chamber. I somehow had the wherewithal to ask the sex of the baby.

"The fetus is a boy," she said in a low whisper.

I got up slowly from my bed and felt the weight of my legs. Every step down the stairs toward my husband took an extreme amount of effort and I felt like a blob of cells moving with no direction. I could still hear the doctor speaking but only in the form of fragmented sentences:

". . .Genetic counselor. . ."
". . .maybe they can get you in on Monday. . ."
". . .you have options. . ."
". . .Potential problems with the fetus. . ."
". . .again, I'm sorry. . ."
". . .questions. . ."
". . .concerns. . ."
". . .risks. . ."

Every word seemed more terrifying than the one before it. I felt like I couldn't breathe and I had the uncontrollable urge to run to some uncharted destination. Somewhere to escape. My body. My mind. The voice on the other end of the phone. I collapsed in a puddle of tears at the bottom of the stairs.

My husband, who was working from home that day, rushed over to me and sat with me on the bottom stair as I sobbed. After what felt like an eternity, I threw the phone down and gathered enough air to blurt out, "They think he has Down syndrome . . . I can't . . . How can we . . . what about my life . . . what about OUR life . . . what about Clay (our older son) . . . I can't do this!"

My husband, often the grounded one in times of heightened emotion, paused for a moment and said gently, "We CAN do this. He is our son and we will love him." With those simple, soft, and succinct words, I calmed down for a millisecond and knew he was right. I knew we already carried so much love in our hearts for this dear boy. But I could feel a dark cloud of fear creeping down over the horizon like lava flowing from an eruption. Slow. Hot. All encompassing.

I curled back into bed and didn't emerge for the entire weekend. The weight of my body was dense and heavy and my mind began to go numb to block out the millions of thoughts. The dissociation was perhaps a defense mechanism to protect me from all the information that had come down like a gavel in a courtroom. A life sentence for a crime I didn't commit.

A few hours after that call, in between crying spells, I saw a clearing from the fog in my mind and remembered a young girl I'd watched onstage, singing "Hello Dolly." Just one night before that fateful call, and two weeks before the entire world shut down from COVID-19, I'd gone to see a high school production with a friend. Midway through the show I noticed a girl who had different features than the other teenagers. Her almond-shaped eyes glistened as she sang and danced along with her fellow performers.

When we left the show that evening I exclaimed, "I'm so impressed the director chose to cast someone with Down syndrome! I've never seen that before! How cool!" I genuinely felt encouraged and filled with hope by the diversity and inclusion I saw reflected on that stage. In all my years of amateur and professional theater, I had not once seen a person with Down syndrome onstage. The whole idea seemed revolutionary to me.

And yet, as I lay in bed the following day, completely paralyzed, mind, body, and soul by my baby's potential diagnosis, I pictured that girl onstage. Where was all that hope I'd felt about her? Why had that vision suddenly diminished? I realized that, in addition to fear, I was grappling with resentment, having already been through so many struggles in 38 years. I considered this another unexpected act in a play I called "My Life." Hadn't I been through enough? A steady stream of emotions filtered through my body 100 miles a minute until one crept in that I hadn't expected and couldn't explain away.

Shame.

Not guilt. Guilt comes from an action that someone does or does not take. I recognized in the early days that nothing I did caused this turn of events. But the shame I felt all throughout my body was all consuming. I wanted this baby. I prayed for this baby. My husband and I intended to have a second child. But the feelings stirring inside of me when the diagnosis was fresh did not align with all of that. I felt like I wanted to run away from my body . . . from this baby . . . from this life. And that made me feel shameful. How could I have gone, in a moment, from celebrating the baby I was carrying to wanting to escape because of the child's potential diagnosis? The darkness that consumed me with those feelings was something I had never experienced before and was more than I could even begin to process, at the time.

Come Monday morning, I finally managed to drag myself out of bed and get ready to meet with the genetic counselor. My husband and I dropped our two-year-old off with a friend and drove to our appointment. A list of questions and worries began to form in my brain as I watched the lifeless, leafless trees whiz past my window, now without a hint of spring budding on their branches.

What would I even ask this person when I met her?

- Did I want to hear what she had to say?
- Would I always feel this alone?
- Would my friends abandon me?
- Were my dreams crushed?
- Is a 9/10 chance as high of a probability as it seemed?
- Was there a loophole in this statistic?

I felt completely desperate and searching as we parked the car in the lot. I was on a relentless merry-go-round of rationalizations and explanations. A sort of "He loves me, he loves me not" dance I was doing in my mind, still desperately trying to make sense of the news we'd been given just two days before. Walking slowly into the building, I noticed a little girl in between her parents. Holding her hands on either side, they were swinging her up and down. I had a flashback to a moment like this with my parents at Disneyland. This is one of the oldest recollections in my memory bank and it gripped me with a sense of nostalgia and a desire for simpler times. As my husband and I passed them, I glanced briefly at the little girl's face.

She had Down syndrome.

I smiled because I don't believe in coincidences.

And then I cried because I don't believe in coincidences.

The hallway leading up to the tiny office felt like an endless sea of white. It was cold and stark with no paintings on the walls. No frills. I felt a little faint as I walked into the room where the genetic counselor stood, welcoming us. Much to my surprise, the woman didn't seem afraid or sorry to see us. She smiled warmly and invited us to sit down.

Without wasting a moment, she began to explain the basics of Down syndrome. It went something like this: "Down syndrome is a genetic condition that occurs when a person has an extra copy of chromosome 21." She showed us a chart that demonstrated the information she was explaining (see Figure 1.1).

"This extra chromosome causes developmental delays and can sometimes make individuals more prone to health concerns. 50% of individuals born with Down syndrome have a heart defect."

As I listened, I could feel the tears primed and ready to flow like Niagara Falls. But instead of continuing to list all the daunting and overwhelming statistics, she shifted gears unpredictably and said, "This occurs randomly at the moment of conception and NOTHING you did caused this or altered the pregnancy. Your baby had this extra chromosome from the very first moment of conception."

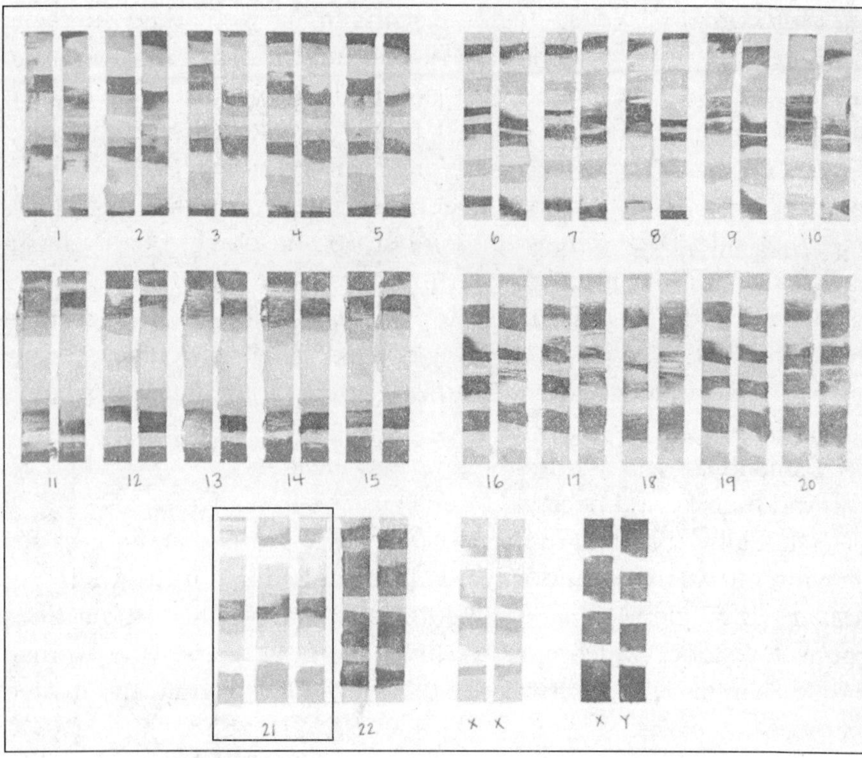

Figure 1.1 Karyotype: An organized profile of a person's chromosomes. This chart shows the extra 21st chromosome characteristic of Down syndrome. Courtesy of Tiffany Abbott Fuller

The genetic counselor handed me some resources (many of the same organizations you will see listed in a chapter in this book)—Jack's Basket, The Down Syndrome Diagnosis Network (DSDN), and a couple of local networks and online support groups to investigate. She shared some statistics about sibling relationships when she learned we had an older son (you'll read about those statistics in Chapter 7). She also shared some quotes from real people with Down syndrome and their love for life (in Chapter 14, you'll read some of their firsthand accounts about living a life with an extra chromosome). The statements she read aloud reflected a brighter view of life than most individuals I've encountered in my lifetime. All of this felt so foreign to me but I slowly began to feel a weight being lifted off my chest. I felt like I could take a baby step forward, into a foreign land.

I had no idea that this newly embarked territory would also include the country shutting down from a global pandemic just a few weeks later. Every doctor's appointment became more daunting and mysterious than the last. My husband couldn't accompany me to any appointments due to lockdown, and there never seemed to be enough masks or hand sanitizer to make me feel safe. I washed my groceries and cleaned boxes that came to the house with gloves on my hands. Nothing seemed steady or certain, and *everything* felt different and more difficult than the day before. The extraordinary magnitude of hardship I went through felt all-encompassing at the time and, reflecting back, I'm not even sure how I got through it. But one baby step at a time, I crept forward. I cried when I needed to cry, I laughed whenever I found something remotely funny, and I tried to hang on to hope. What hope, I didn't know.

About seven months into my pregnancy, my friends threw me a baby shower over Zoom. Twenty-five or thirty people came and we all gushed being together, since we'd been so deprived of human connection for months during the pandemic. I relished the laughter; I allowed the tears to fall slowly down my face as I honestly expressed my fears about this precious baby. Would he be ok? Would I be ok? Would our family be ok?

But in this call, I also found hope wrapping itself around my heart like a glove in a way it hadn't before. In the midst of the hope I was feeling, I had a sudden flashback to watching *FROZEN II* with my son, shortly after the call I'd received from the doctor. The character Anna found herself in uncharted waters and sang a song that described exactly how I felt. The final verse said:

> With the dawn, what comes then
>
> When it's clear that everything will never be the same again?
>
> Then I'll make the choice
>
> To hear that voice
>
> And do the NEXT—RIGHT—THING.

The "next right thing" had indeed carried me through my pregnancy to the moment of my Zoom celebration and all the way up to Jedidiah's birth . . .

. . . but we'll get to that.

A Little Extra

As I write this, I'm picturing a woman who received word from her doctor about the child in her belly. I'm envisioning the mom and dad who are sitting in a dark hospital room with a birth diagnosis after a lot of whispering and side glances. I can see the single mom who has been juggling so many things already, and now she has to figure out how to balance and immerse herself in an all-encompassing land of early intervention and appointments with specialists. I wish I could hug every person who did *NOT* have the positive experience with their genetic counselor that my husband and I experienced.

In my correspondence with hundreds of families through my platform, Happiness Is Down Syndrome, I've heard about the terrible bedside manner that often accompanies a diagnosis. The fear and grief that can follow those moments are *REAL* and *SACRED* and not unusual. I traveled to Armenia with an organization called RODS Heroes (you'll hear more about them, later) and met with mothers who had lost their whole support system, including their husbands, simply because they chose to keep their baby with Down syndrome and not give the child up for adoption. I stood face-to-face with a mother from India and another from Ghana after giving a speech at the UN who told me about their unique challenges in their respective countries. No two journeys are the same, yet we can relate to one another in a powerful way when given the opportunities and proper tools to do so.

CHAPTER 2

Diagnosis Story Diaries

"We don't heal in isolation, but in community."
—S. Kelley Harrell

Walking out of the meeting with our genetic counselor, I clutched a folder full of resources tightly to my body, as if my very survival depended on it. I remember feeling an odd combination of hope and immense overwhelm. My mind continued to reel, and I struggled to envision my life with this baby. In fact, I had a hard time picturing a baby at all. All I could hold on to was a diagnosis about which I knew almost nothing. A diagnosis of unknowns was front and center, making it virtually impossible for me to even begin to picture the little person he would be once he was born. And when I started to, I was afraid of the visual that popped into my head. And the pictures that would pop up in a Google search? Forget about it! They were terrifying and not helpful in the slightest.

These were some of the questions that circled around in my brain like a continuous hamster wheel:

- *What if he doesn't talk?*
- *When will he walk?*
- *What if he has a dual diagnosis?*
- *What if he's one of the 50% of children with Down syndrome born with a heart defect?*

- *Who am I to raise this child? I know NOTHING about disability. How will I do it?*
- *What if someone tells me something about their child that is too triggering?*
- *What if people make fun of him or shun him?*

These questions and concerns I experienced in the early days are not uncommon. Many people aren't ready to read anything about Down syndrome, let alone talk to families in the community. For those families, organizations like Jack's Basket can bring hope from afar to land on your doorstep. These baskets can look like a beacon of light in a land that often feels like isolation and darkness. And it all started with a mother who was filled with fear upon receiving her own son's diagnosis.

Spreading Light on an Unexpected Path

By Carissa L. Carroll, M. Ed, Founder and CEO of Jack's Basket

"When my son Jack was born, his Down syndrome diagnosis left me consumed by fear and uncertainty. I questioned how it would change my family and me, and the unfamiliar journey ahead weighed heavily on my mind. Would I be strong enough to navigate this new reality? But as I moved through those first overwhelming months, I discovered that the best resources were the connections I made with other parents and, most importantly, the lessons I learned from Jack himself. He became my greatest teacher, showing me that love, acceptance, and embracing the unexpected would be the guiding lights on our journey.

The idea for Jack's Basket sparked when I met another mother who shared a heartbreaking diagnosis story of how her baby's Down syndrome diagnosis was delivered in a harsh, impersonal way similar to my own experience. She deserved better and so did her baby. Her story mirrored so many others I had heard, and I knew it was time to change the way families received this news. Every child deserves to be celebrated, and every family should hear 'congratulations,' not 'I'm sorry.'

This realization drove me to create Jack's Basket on Jack's first birthday, starting with delivering gift baskets to new parents. These baskets, filled with gifts, resources, and personal stories, would become a symbol of celebration and hope. The broader Down syndrome community, along with the families we serve through Jack's Basket, has been an invaluable source of strength. Since 2014, we've celebrated nearly 12,000 babies across 50 states and 55 countries, and this community continues to grow, offering support, understanding, and shared experiences. Connecting with other parents and advocates has shown me that, while the journey may be filled with unexpected experiences, we are never alone.

Through Jack's Basket, we've also created a space where families can feel celebrated, supported, and understood. In addition, our work with medical providers, training them to deliver diagnoses with compassion and without bias, has been an important part of changing the way Down syndrome is introduced to families. The collective power of the Down syndrome community, as well as the connections built within Jack's Basket, gives me hope every day that we can continue to create a world where all individuals are seen for their worth and potential. The journey you are about to embark on may be filled with unexpected experiences, but it will also be full of moments of joy, learning, and growth. Your child will teach you lessons you never imagined, opening your heart in ways you never thought possible. They are a gift, and their presence in your life will help you see the world through a new, more compassionate lens. Congratulations!"

Reactions to a diagnosis can be as varied and vast as the stars in the sky. Some families don't feel any sadness over the diagnosis, only surprise. In contrast, there are parents who are a few months or even years into raising their child with Down syndrome and still have trouble accepting their reality. There is no wrong way to walk this path. Do your very best to suspend judgment on yourself. Quite often, denial can be a *huge* part of the first days into a diagnosis and grace upon grace upon grace is needed.

For me, it took research and community to begin to emerge from the dark cloud I was under.

I slowly began immersing myself in the world of Down syndrome and educating myself about the diagnosis. Initially, a quick Wikipedia search of "What is Down syndrome" led me to some basic facts and, as I dove in further, I learned about the National Down Syndrome Society (NDSS). This organization was a wealth of knowledge where I learned that Down syndrome is the most common chromosomal abnormality and that it occurs in about 1 in 1,000 babies born worldwide and 1 in 700 in the United States. In 2015, there were 5.4 million people with Down syndrome globally. The syndrome is named after British physician John Langdon Down, who dedicated his medical practice to the cause.

I learned that there are three different genetic forms of Down syndrome that have been identified:

- The most common is Trisomy 21, involving an extra copy of chromosome 21 in all cells.
- Translocation Down syndrome involves attachment of an extra chromosome in 21 material.
- Mosaic Down syndrome affects some of the cells in the body but not all.

Down syndrome life expectancy has increased primarily due to medical advancements, particularly in treating congenital heart defects, coupled with improved healthcare access and management of related conditions. According to an article written in early 2025 by Brian Chicoine, MD, Medical Director of the Adult Down Syndrome Center:

> "People with Down syndrome are living longer and healthier than any other time in the past. In 1900, the life expectancy of people with Down syndrome was 9 years. By 1984, the life

> expectancy had increased to 28 years. Since then, the life expectancy of people with Down syndrome has increased to about 60 years in white individuals in the United States. The increase in life expectancy is attributed largely to advances in cardiac surgery and in general health management. Approximately 50% of infants with Down syndrome are born with congenital heart disease, and the accessibility of surgical correction has greatly reduced deaths related to congenital heart disease. While there are some racial differences in life expectancy of people with Down syndrome, the differences appear to be decreasing. In 1950, the life expectancy of non-Hispanic Blacks was 22 years (mean) and 4 years (median). In 2010, the life expectancy of non-Hispanic Blacks was 50 (mean) and 57 (median). The life expectancy of non-Hispanic whites was 54 (mean) and 58 (median) in 2010. We had the privilege to meet one of the oldest well-documented people with Down syndrome, a woman with Down syndrome who died at age 82 years. While living into the 70s is still not common for people with Down syndrome, there are more reports of individuals with Down syndrome living that long."[1]

With medical advancements, improved support and healthcare, early intervention, and increased advocacy work for individuals with Down syndrome, the life expectancy and quality of life have greatly increased. Organizations like NDSS, NDSC, Global Down Syndrome, and others are leading the charge in paving a more hope-filled road for families walking this path.

As I gathered information and saw the steady and encouraging scientific progression, I began the slow road to fully accepting the idea that my child most likely would be born with Down syndrome. Being an all or nothing kind of person I said to myself, "Misty, you can continue to curl up in bed, hide from reality, neglect your son and husband, and just resolve to die or you can dive head first into community and support." I'm so thankful I chose the latter. I signed in to a local mom chat on social media and wrote a post about what was going on in my life. I was desperate to find someone—ANYONE—who could guide me toward the light. One mother of a child with Down syndrome saw that post and offered to speak with me on the phone.

While I desperately craved connection, I was hesitant to speak with her at first because it made everything feel so much more real. Eventually, I gathered the courage to call her. It wasn't easy dialing the phone number of a stranger having NO idea what I would hear on the other end. But the moment she picked up, I knew I had made the right decision. She sounded joy-filled . . . even . . . happy. I couldn't believe it. She spoke about the genuine love she felt for her child and told me she wouldn't change a hair on his head. As strange as that sounded to me, I believed her.

I began to see a flicker of light.

I continued to pick up the phone to call friends and family who may have encountered someone with Down syndrome. I vividly remember a conversation with my close friend from high school whose voice never wavered when he said, "Misty, a friend of mine has a daughter with Down syndrome and she sang in a talent show I went to see. She was really good. She lit up the stage." Although it was difficult for me to wrap my head around that at the time, the ease with which he shared this story bred hope inside of me . . . "A person with Down syndrome singing? Wow!" Aside from the young woman with Down syndrome I had seen performing on stage the day before my diagnosis, I would never have envisioned such a thing. Now, five years later, I am dear friends with a young lady with Down syndrome named Mia Rodriguez who uses her gift of music to sing and light up the stage everywhere she goes. She and her wonderful family are sounding boards for my own family and you'll hear from them later in this book.

Shortly after the conversation with my friend, my pastor gave me the number of a couple who had raised a daughter with Down syndrome and I decided to call them, as well. Two hours later, I began to see a bigger, steady light that was no longer flickering. Though their daughter had passed away in her thirties due to some health complications, this couple had a similar, joy-filled tone to their voices and shared about the happiness Lisa brought to them while she was on Earth. Craig and Lori remain a huge source of support to my family, today. There are a myriad of ways to find close connections like this through local and national organizations.

Gaining footing, I joined a Birth Group with the Down Syndrome Diagnosis Network (the DSDN) full of mothers who were also pregnant with babies who had Down syndrome in the middle of a global pandemic. I began to connect on a personal level with 1 . . . 2 . . . 5 . . . 10 . . . 20 . . . 50 women all over the country. I began to feel a part of something bigger and grasped the fact that I WAS NOT alone. I then connected with a local GiGi's Playhouse and found that there are SO many ways to learn and grow with support. (Check out Chapter 16 to learn more.)

I began to see light filling up the whole room, at this point.

It didn't happen overnight but slowly and steadily, day by day, my mindset shifted. My heart softened. My eyes opened. I began to see that this wasn't just about *me*. Poor me. Woe is me. Why me?! This was about WE. It was about moving from *me* to *we*. Many people were facing a future similar to mine and we were stronger together. We were able to brave the next minute and do the next right thing. Together, sharing our struggles and victories, we could face the next hour. The next day. The rest of our pregnancy.

And when Jedidiah Coy Snyder was born on August 1, 2020, I have never felt more like a *we* than I did when I held him. All of my fears that were centered on *me* completely transformed into *we*! I whispered softly in his ear, "No matter what, Jed, *we* will face this together. *We* will see this through. *We've* got this!" I held him in my arms and felt my heart and mind expand exponentially. It felt like my eyes were completely open for the first time and I could see pieces and faces and places I'd never seen before. New colors and hues. New sounds and dynamics. It felt like all throughout my life, I had been walking along looking for *one* destination. *One* predictable, safe spot was along the path. But as I was walking, I came upon a secret garden. I hadn't been looking for it and I certainly didn't want to stop to look inside . . . but once I *did* find it and *did* look inside, there was a whole new world of color. A whole new world of people . . . a whole new world of beauty.

Finding people and organizations to walk the path with you is key. Community paves the way to opportunity. Opportunity paves the way to inclusion, education, exposure, and ultimately, *acceptance*. Not just an acceptance of an unexpected diagnosis but an acceptance of the unique qualities of every person you come across in life. Down syndrome has burst open so many doors and I find myself saying to those behind me in the journey, "Hey, come on into the garden! Join us. There is so much to see and learn here."

Parents are not meant to teach, guide, and educate their children alone, on an island.

- If your child wants to learn to tap dance, you may send them to a class.
- When your child wants to master a certain sport, you may find them a coach.
- When your child surpasses your knowledge in a certain subject, you may hire a tutor.
- When your child is sick, you may send them to a physician or a nutritionist.

If these things are permissible and encouraged, why are so many parents in the disability community holding themselves to impossible standards in our daily lives? Why do we think we have to white knuckle it and do it alone? So many of us are expecting ourselves to be experts in fields others have trained for their entire lives. I've seen this tendency in myself and so many of those around me.

I've seen a temptation to try to become overnight experts in subjects we've never studied before. A propensity to overload ourselves with "to-dos" for our kids when there are so many ways and reasons to unload tasks onto our community or just take them off the list for the time being. There is often a compulsion to do more, be more, strive more when it comes to our kids and so many other facets of our lives.

Why?

We weren't ever meant to be any person's end-all, be-all.

At one of Jed's first checkups with the pediatrician, she took one look at my exhausted, tear-stained eyes and said, "Misty, I'm only going to give you a short checklist of to-do's for Jed. We are going to take things one appointment, one day at a time. The most pressing things first. Rome wasn't built in a day."

Likewise, understanding a new community doesn't happen overnight. It's built slowly, brick by brick. Ultimately we discover that we are stronger, together. As our pediatrician said to me, we can choose to show up in the world, one day at a time, one support page at a time, one appointment at a time, one advocacy campaign at a time.

We don't need to have all the answers or an entire community of besties at our disposal. But we SHOULD seek to find a group of people who are experiencing commonalities that can help make the path seem a little less daunting and a little more clear. Whenever I speak with parents who struggle with depression and disillusionment many years after their child is born, the through line seems to be a lack of community. I hope this encourages you to find some people to accompany you along this path.

A Little Extra

In connecting with parents all throughout the globe, I've encountered many parents who are simply not ready to find community until well after the baby is born. *That is ok*! We all have different timelines, and no two people are the same. However, I encourage everyone to observe a page like Happiness is Down syndrome on social media, which I created for parents to come and see the joy and love experienced in families like ours.

There is also a community Facebook page for friends, families, and allies in the Down syndrome community called Extra Community. Come and join it! You can be a fly on the wall, and you don't have to participate in any way if you aren't ready to do that. Exposure and awareness is key. We all have hidden bias and ableism deep within us and the more we can peel back those layers, the easier it will be to accept a diagnosis in your own child.

CHAPTER 3

Space for Grief and Acceptance

> *"Before you were born I carried you under my heart. From the moment you arrived in this world until the moment I leave it, I will always carry you in my heart."*
>
> —Mandy Harrison

Since Jed was born in 2020, I've done a lot of boots on the ground, grassroots, person-to-person research of my own. After these conversations or written accounts, I've made a point of documenting and noting the similarities of these stories. Some of these parallels include:

- The news is shared with a grim or abrasive tone.
- "I'm sorry" is often uttered.
- There are few resources offered and little to no follow-up.
- The whole experience is shrouded in fear and sadness.
- The "risks" are covered in detail, but the light of Down syndrome often is not.

Whether receiving a prenatal or birth diagnosis, unexpected news during pregnancy can feel like a freight train coming at you, full speed. Because my pregnancy was tumultuous and swimming with stressful unknowns after I received the 9/10 probability, I often agonized over my choice to do prenatal testing, wishing I had opted out. The only reason I decided to get noninvasive prenatal testing (NIPT) was to find out the sex of the baby. This pregnancy felt vastly different than my first and, because of that, I was convinced I was having a girl. Before running out to buy pink frills and bows, I wanted to make sure my instinct was correct. I had no idea, at the time, that I was opting to hear the news that would change the tone of my entire pregnancy and the trajectory of my life. From the time I answered that call from the doctor at 14 weeks until the moment Jed was born, my thoughts were consumed by fear and, what I now understand was, deep grief.

I was ill-equipped to recognize and tackle this grief at the time, but I have since met others on the journey who are skilled and insightful about how overpowering it can be for a newly diagnosed family. Elizabeth Wofford is one of the helpful resources I've found. She is a licensed professional, counselor, educator, and researcher whose work centers on the lived experience of parents navigating medical complexity and unexpected diagnoses. She has worked as a counselor for nearly a decade and has been trained in various trauma modalities such as EMDR and Brainspotting.

As both a clinician and a mother to a son with Down syndrome, she has walked through her own seasons of grief, uncertainty, and hope. She brings a deeply compassionate understanding to the emotional journey families face during pregnancy. Elizabeth specializes in trauma and working with parents of children with medically complex issues, and her writing and teaching reflect her commitment to helping parents feel seen, supported, and empowered. When I asked her what she would like to share with this community, she was generous enough to share her personal and professional experience!

Guilt, Shame, and the Hidden Weight of Grief

By Elizabeth Wofford, PhD, LPC/S

Guilt says, "I did something bad." Shame says, "I am bad" (something is wrong with me). Grief, and trauma, when not understood, can lead to shame.

How the Brain Makes Sense of the World: Mental Maps and Schemas

Our brains or organs of prediction. Their job is to learn about our world and begin to predict things. It builds mental maps, or what psychologists call schemas, when I do this, X happens. When they do that, Y happens. If I want Z, I must do A and B. We begin forming these understandings as young children and go through constant processes of revising and editing these maps. That's what learning is—adjusting our maps.

Assimilation and Accommodation: When New Information Doesn't Fit

In the early 1900s when cognitive theorists were beginning to describe how we learn, Jean Piaget studied how we learn and described many amazing aspects of the human mind.[1] There are two processes that are critical to understand in how we adjust our mental maps, assimilation and accommodation. When we get new information, sometimes it fits into and expands what we already know: that's assimilation. But sometimes that new information is different enough from what we know that we must change our map, or even build a new one: that's accommodation.

When Pregnancy Doesn't Follow the Map: My Story

For example, I have had two pregnancies. As my second pregnancy began, I experienced slightly different symptoms with my second pregnancy than I had with my first. However, both fell into the realm of what I expected could happen, so my mind easily assimilated that information. When pregnant with my daughter, I experienced significant meat aversion, but not generalized nausea; with my pregnancy with my son, I was nauseous all the time. But there were other aspects of pregnancy that differed so drastically that I could not assimilate the information.

(*continued*)

At 13 weeks pregnant, some routine screening took an unexpected turn when we were told that not only was my son likely to have Down Syndrome, he also had other issues that meant the pregnancy itself might not be viable. My husband and I sat in shock. Our mental maps had NO frame of reference for this information. We sat in a weekend of limbo while we waited for the results of genetic testing and some answers, while having to wrestle with the idea that many answers were not even possible to find. It was all a game of "wait and see."

All of a sudden, what we expected about pregnancy, or having a child, was gone. Our mental maps failed. We didn't even know where to go to get new maps. This no-man's land when expectations fail can be disorienting to say the least. Often it leaves us in a storm in a sea with no land or life raft in sight. Our brains don't know what to do. That's why you are reading this book. I want to share with you some about my experiences with my ocean, Grief, and how we begin to build roads back to our mental maps.

Understanding the Assumptive World: The Foundation of Our Expectations

To understand grief, we have to first recognize the maps and assumptions that we operate on in all aspects of our lives. This is termed the "assumptive world" and is a term that is credited to John Bowlby, the father of attachment theory. Attachment theory describes how we form relationships and meet needs for love and connection. So it's only natural that he also identified how grief is connected to the same systems that build attachment. Grief comes when we lose the thing we had, or thought we had. Attachment is built on patterns of interactions and responses, which build expectations. A baby cries, and is fed by a parent; this happens repeatedly that the baby comes to know that when they cry, the parent will help. This is secure attachment. The baby now has a mental map that says I know that crying will bring the help of the people I love and who love me.[2,3]

Identifying Our Assumptions: "This Isn't How It Was Supposed to Go"

We build our entire way of being in the world on assumptions, and they tend to fall into three main categories: what we believe about ourselves, others, and the world. They set up mental maps for how we expect things to go, and expect things to work. We often don't see these assumptions until they are disrupted. Have you ever caught yourself shocked by something and saying "Oh my goodness, that's just now how that was supposed to go?"—you just found one of your assumptions in your map. We build maps of how people should treat us, how we should act, and what we do to keep ourselves healthy and safe. We build maps that tell us if the world is a safe place, if we can trust others, and what we believe about ourselves.

Our brain cannot process every single piece of every day and moment; it runs on assumptions and follows formerly followed paths until something comes along to interrupt us. Then we have to decide what to do next. There is nothing wrong with these assumptions. But sometimes, they are so drastically disrupted that we feel that our worlds are turned upside down. When our assumptions and expectations are disruptive, violated, or destroyed, we can feel "deeply vulnerable and unsafe, because the world that we once knew, the world we once relied on, and the images and perceptions of ourselves may prove to be no longer relevant in light of what we have experienced."[4]

What Grief Really Is: A Normal Adaptive Response

Grief is the response when those assumptions are disrupted, violated, or completely erased. The actual definition of grief is an adaptive process, not a pathology, the normal, natural response to loss. And believe it or not, the point of grief, is to help us build new assumptions and a new assumptive world. When your map has just been rendered completely useless and you find yourself in new territory with no frame of reference,

(*continued*)

grief is actually where you need to begin. Nursing literature defines grief this way: "A normal, complex process that includes emotional, physical, spiritual, social, and intellectual responses and behaviors by which individuals, families, and communities incorporate an actual, anticipated, or perceived loss into their daily lives."

Many of us have considered grief in terms of death and permanent loss, but you might be asking how grief applies to us if someone has not died? There are so many more types of grief than many of us have ever heard of, and they can overlap and operate at the same time in many situations. The list below gives an abbreviated summary of what we call "non-death losses" and other types of grief. Every single type of grief affects our assumptive world.

- Non-Death Loss—Losses unrelated to death, such as health, function, identity, or relationships.
- Anticipatory Grief—Grieving that begins before an expected loss occurs.
- Traumatic Grief—Grief following a sudden, violent, or traumatic loss.
- Secondary Loss—The chain reaction of additional losses that follow the primary one.
- Ambiguous Loss—Loss that lacks clarity; the person may be physically present but psychologically absent, or vice versa.
- Non-Finite Loss—Ongoing, changing, and uncertain losses with no clear end point.
- Cumulative Grief—Experiencing multiple losses over time, often without space to recover or process between them.
- Collective Grief—Shared grief experienced by groups or communities after a large-scale or shared loss.
- Disenfranchised Grief—Grief that is not recognized, validated, or socially supported by others.

How Non-Death Loss Connects to Identity and Attachment

When we consider non-death loss and attachment, it can sometimes be a challenge to identify what it was that we were attached to that we might have lost, or partially lost. Harris and Winokuer (2019) note that "it could be that these defining, overarching losses involve either the loss of an aspect of ourselves to which we are attached or to our place in the world, which makes us feel safe and secure" (p. 123). We have to begin to identify the types of grief and the assumptions, expectations, and attachments at play before we can begin to rebuild our world.

My Experience: Multiple Layers of Grief at Once

When I learned that my son likely had Down Syndrome, and that he may not even survive his pregnancy, many types of grief began operating at once. Anticipatory grief, as I did not know what was coming but I was told loss was coming one way or another. I could lose the pregnancy and a child, or if he survived, I could lose any picture of "having a son" that I may have previously held. Ambiguous loss was at work, because there was so much uncertainty and unknown. When assumptions are violated it creates uncertainty, and often fear. We know something "isn't right" and this "isn't how it's supposed to be" but we don't always even know where to begin in grieving because we don't know what we are actually grieving. My son might live, he might walk, he might talk, he might do all the things I expect a son would do. Or he might not. I don't know, and I won't know until we get there.

While grief and trauma are related concepts, they are not the same. Trauma is anything that overwhelms our ability to cope and challenges our sense of safety, control, and predictability.[5] Not all grief is traumatic, but in my case, I also experienced traumatic grief, as the threat of death loss loomed over us and all the things that might come with that, including possible health risks for me, created some trauma. The doctor's office was now a place I dreaded because I didn't know when the next "shoe would drop."

(*continued*)

I also had cumulative grief at work, because I was processing the possibility of a diagnosis of Down syndrome but the other conditions, they thought he had included other things like possible severe heart defects, brain damage, and others. Every single one of those brings its own set of violated and shattered expectations. I also was experiencing disenfranchised grief, I had well meaning, but unhelpful people saying things like:

> "Oh don't go there yet, you don't know that it will be xyz."
> "But children with Down syndrome are such a joy, that isn't a death sentence."

Even though these things might have been factually true, they completely invalidated my grief. It is like trying to put a band-aid on a gaping wound without first addressing the wound. That's a lot.

Starting from Scratch: Rebuilding a World That Doesn't Feel Familiar

Shattered assumptions can rip a gaping hole in the fabric of our lives. Many times we are starting from scratch to find our footing and begin to rebuild. So if it feels like your world is in shambles around you, it might be because it is. And that's ok. You may be asking questions about who you are (how can I be a special needs mom), about others (how will others respond, will they love my child too, will they misunderstand my child?) and the world (will he be able to get a job? How will he do in school if he is different from his peers, etc.). We may be able to assimilate some things into our assumptive worlds, but not others. Each person is unique, and has their own mental map, and so the thing that would be hard for you to assimilate into your set of expectations may not be hard for me at all. Your history is different from mine. Your map was built on different expectations.

When I learned that I had a thyroid condition and would need thyroid medicine for the rest of my life, that was easy to assimilate for me. I knew what was going on, I had explanations for things I could not previously understand (all my random symptoms), and I knew a lot about my health, and this fit right into my mental map of how to better manage my health. However, when I learned that my son had Down Syndrome, I had very little frame of reference for that. I wracked my brain and found only two things about Down Syndrome in my set of assumptions: (1) I had been taught that it happened when mothers were too old (not true!), and (2) I was scared of being around people with Down Syndrome because I'd never been taught how to relate to them. That mental map was not going to work for me anymore.

Naming Assumptions Without Shame

To begin adjusting and rebuilding assumptions, we often have to start by naming the ones we already have. Often we are ashamed when we hear our own thoughts, and we don't realize that they are built on previous experiences, or things we have been taught, they are not always our own thoughts and don't represent our character and who we are. When grief is not understood, or is often misunderstood, it can lead to shame. We don't know why we are reacting a certain way, so we assume that we must be bad or broken. And it's not true. You are just lost and need a new map. The grieving process is the way in which we rebuild assumptions and create new meanings. To do this, we must walk day by day, moment by moment, through the journey of finding these expectations, and either assimilating our experience into something we already understand, or building new understandings. This process can be exhausting. In the same way that young children can be tired after a long day of learning at school, we are being constantly assaulted and bombarded with "yet another thing" that isn't going like we thought it would. When grief layers upon itself, it can knock us down and we may feel like we will never come up for air.

(*continued*)

The Ocean of Grief: Learning to Ride the Waves

One of the popular analogies for grief in the counseling world is that of an ocean and waves. Grief is not a pathology, a sickness, or a disease. It is not the result of something that is broken. It is a natural process that will ebb and flow. Some days the waves are calm. Gentle wind will cause the waves to lap the shore gently. These things bump into our assumptions but are easy to ride out, and we are used to the rhythm. The longer you learn your grief process the more comfortable you become with knowing how you personally respond to waves.

Some days the surf is choppier. It doesn't rise above your knees but it hits with some force, and you never know which wave is going to be stronger than the others. You brace yourself and still feel off balance. Other days, the waves are of epic proportion. They knock you down, and sometimes pull you under. They keep coming, wave after wave. Unfortunately you can't make them stop. But you can learn how to swim. You can learn to give yourself freedom to grieve and experience the overwhelming, unrelenting pain, sadness, anger, or any other of many emotions that may be swirling around you. You can know that the waves will change eventually. The calm times may seem forever away, but even in the midst of the storms and chaos, if you begin this process of naming your expectations and your grief, you get to know it. You begin to build your boat. You learn what helps you most with each kind of wave.

For me, with the big waves, I just have to cry. I need to stop googling, sometimes I want to be alone, sometimes I want to cry with a friend, but I just have to acknowledge how big the waves are. How much I don't know. I don't know if my son will ever talk, I grieve the moments of mother-son conversations I just assumed I would have. I hold space for that loss. I make space for that loss. I will have other types of moments with my son. I know that, but it doesn't replace what I might lose. And for those who try to comfort us, if they try to reassure us that things will "get better" or "not be that bad" without acknowledging all that we feel that we have lost, they can often hurt more than help. Which leaves us feeling more alone and lost.

When we begin to name our grief, we also have to find ways to understand how it affects us. Grief can impact all aspects of life and shows up physically, psychologically, socially, spiritually, economically, and practically (Harris & Winokuer, 2019).

How Grief Shows Up in the Body, Mind, and Daily Life

Grief impacts individuals physically, psychologically, socially, spiritually, economically, and practically. Psychologically, it can manifest as intense sadness, anxiety, and difficulty concentrating. Physically, grief can lead to fatigue, sleep disturbances, headaches, and digestive issues. Socially, people may withdraw or become irritable, while practically, day-to-day functioning can be impaired. Spiritually, it may lead to questioning beliefs, and economically, it can cause financial stress or impact work performance.

- Psychologically: thoughts, feelings, and emotions

  Intense sadness, anxiety, guilt, emotional numbness, intrusive thoughts, difficulty concentrating, difficulty making decisions[6,7,8]
- Physically: bodily symptoms

  Fatigue, headaches, muscle tension, appetite changes, gastrointestinal distress, chest tightness, sleep disturbances, weakened immune functioning[9,10,11]
- Socially: changes in interpersonal dynamics and social expectations, withdrawal from others, loneliness, feeling misunderstood, role changes, reduced social support over time[12,13,14]
- Spiritually: a quest for meaning or existential suffering, questioning beliefs, anger toward God, struggling with meaning, deepening or shifting faith practices[15,16,17]
- Economically: changes in financial status and expenses incurred after loss, funeral and medical expenses, productivity decreases, job disruption, loss of household income[18,19,20]

(*continued*)

- Practically: changes in day-to-day routine as a result of a loss difficulty maintaining routines, impaired task completion, reduced ability to manage responsibilities, decreased work or school performance[21,22,23]

I wish I had known Elizabeth at the time of my pregnancy to more fully grasp the inner workings of grief. I'm confident that there are readers who will be able to cling to even one or two lines above and know that there is complex emotion involved in what they are going through. Awareness is key, and when we are aware of what is going on internally, we can begin to heal and progress.

Some families hold tightly to a small percentage of a chance that their child will not be born with Down syndrome. Especially when friends and family members tend to share stories like, "I had a friend who was told their baby would have Down syndrome and the test was wrong!" While it may feel comforting in the early days of a diagnosis to entertain that idea, it's important to remember that testing is not the same today as it was 20, 15, 10 or even a few years ago.

According to the website 3 Billion, noninvasive prenatal testing (NIPT) has a high sensitivity, which means it is very good at correctly identifying cases where a chromosomal abnormality is present. For common trisomies like Down syndrome (Trisomy 21), Edwards syndrome (Trisomy 18), and Patau syndrome (Trisomy 13), NIPT often has a sensitivity of over 99%.[24] It's important to remember this when clinging to any idea about whether or not a diagnosis is accurate without an amniocentesis or Chorionic villus sampling that can verify with 100% certainty.

Erin, a mother in the Down syndrome community, shares her thoughts about her prenatal diagnosis.

An Unexpected Turn of Events

Erin Eicher, Mom to Maverick and Advocate in the Down syndrome community

At 46 years old, the thought of another child was the last thing on my mind. After years of infertility, two of my children were conceived with help from both the medical field and naturopathic help, with our middle child being adopted at 10 months old. Our kids were ages 18, 12, & 7 when, after a date night, my husband suggested we get a pregnancy test. I took the test only for it to come out positive right away. I could not believe what I was seeing. I was not trying or hoping to get pregnant. We didn't think we could conceive on our own after so many years of not using birth control, and we had only been successful at conceiving when we were seeking help. Everything switched that evening and our thoughts turned to the future and what it would mean to start over again with a baby. At first I was a bit confused and a little irritated at the timing.

When I was in my 20s and 30s I begged God for children and we sought all sorts of treatment to try and get pregnant to no avail. I was content that I had been able to conceive twice and adopt once, I was fulfilled.

Why now was the prayer from so many years ago, to conceive naturally, being answered?

We couldn't understand it. After working through the initial shock and irritation we began to get excited. I felt great being pregnant and things were so good. Until one ultrasound showed a slightly inflamed kidney. My midwife said this is common in boys and could mean nothing at all. However, it was also considered a soft marker for Down Syndrome so if we wanted to test for that we could. My husband did not want the test because of course it changed nothing about our love and desire for our baby. I wanted the test done just so I could know what was going on. I was sure it would be nothing.

About 10 days later I got a call from our midwife on May 13, 2022, time seemed to stop when she said the words, "Is your husband home too?" I knew she was calling with news she was nervous to give. My husband was not home but I took the call anyway. She said the blood test showed a 95/100% chance that our little boy would have Down Syndrome. I remember her saying something about "these kids are filled with so much joy" and thinking that's a strange thing to tell me right now when all I can think of is my world is crashing down. We got off the

(*continued*)

phone and I ran to my room to be alone. We were hosting my Mom and cousin who were in town from NY for my oldest son's graduation party. I wasn't sure I wanted to tell anyone or even how I felt, my head was swirling. I texted my husband and told him what the midwife said and all he wrote back was, "Wow." He came home soon after and I stayed in my room that night. I couldn't face anyone. I cried and I cried. It felt so mean of God to allow me to get pregnant when I wasn't asking, when I was 46 and then give us a child with a disability.

The next day was my oldest son's graduation party. I had to put on a smile and go through the day as though all was fine. We had a great day with him and it was a good distraction. But when evening came and quietness came, a flood of emotions came. I felt stuck in my body, stuck with a life plan that wasn't mine. It felt like it was someone else's and I was being forced down a road I didn't want to go. The first weeks after hearing the news it was like I tried to escape my reality in my mind but my big baby belly and wiggling infant inside wouldn't let me escape it. I felt myself detaching from him, I didn't want to put my hand on my belly anymore. Almost like I was mad he existed and that it was his fault for making me do something I didn't want to do. I began to realize how unhealthy this mindset was and how it wasn't good for me or the baby. Only close friends and family knew about this new twist and I knew they were praying for me.

I believe in the power of prayer and I believe it was those prayers that helped me out of the darkness I was feeling in my mind. I decided to write out some affirmations over me and the baby. Things like:

"My son is a gift from God"
"I have a good attachment to him"
"My baby will be born on the exact day set aside for his birth"
"My baby is healthy and strong"

These and a few others I would speak over myself and the baby every night before going to bed. Slowly my heart began to change and I felt excited to meet him again. I enjoyed his kicks and movements and reveled in the fact that I got to be pregnant again and at 46 years old! His birth was amazing, in a tub with quietness and me following my body's lead and my husband by my side. He came out and when I looked at him I knew it wasn't 95%, it was 100%; he had Down syndrome. All I could think of was "I'm sorry." I'm sorry I was mad about you, I'm sorry I was scared about you, I'm sorry I doubted.

He was small at 6lbs 10oz but he was strong. He had no health issues and began nursing that first night. Fast forward 2 ½ years and while I still have tears now and then, I have many more smiles and laughter. It's been a journey that has looked different than we thought. It's not a journey that has been easy but it's worth it. He is worth it. When I see the light my son brings to this world I have a feeling God has big plans for him. Bigger ones than I can imagine. There is a purpose and reason for a 46-year-old woman and 48-year-old man to have had another child who came with 47 chromosomes. There is a purpose greater than us!

In addition to community support and online chats like the ones I found with the Down Syndrome Diagnosis Network (DSDN) and the ones I created through Happiness is Down syndrome and Extra Community, there are a lot of moms like Erin on social media who allow the world to walk with them through the daily ups and downs of their pregnancy. If you are willing to seek out pages like this, you will find similar struggles and triumphs to your own, along with a personal connection with the person who is posting, in real time. It's one of the beauties of social media.

The struggle with a diagnosis is not foreign to any particular parent or caregiver. It's common to grieve the life you thought you would be living. Mom Amanda, with a background in social work, still had difficulty processing her prenatal diagnosis.

From Lecture Halls to Hospital Walls

By Amanda Ellard, Mom in the Down syndrome community, Advocate, Social worker

It's like muscle memory—the reminder of what it feels like in that split second when your life becomes a "before" and "after." I can remember the smell of the building, the sound of squeaky shoes in the hallway. . . the way my ponytail was giving me a headache. I remember the lights that were way too bright, and the room that felt way too small. And I remember the words that she said with such unceremonious certainty—as if they weren't actively shattering every version of myself that I'd ever known. "The results are positive. You have an 87% likelihood of your baby having Down Syndrome. I'm sorry. Do you want to know the sex? It's a girl." And just like that, I'd become the after.

Suddenly I found myself living in a world where every breath I took, every choice I made, they all were done as the mommy of a little girl with Down syndrome. It felt foreign and wrong; like looking in the mirror and not recognizing the reflection looking back at you. And it felt lonely. In desperation, I immediately turned to social media, hoping that I could find someone—anyone—who could relate to what I was feeling. Instead, I found post after post of women shouting the worth and value of their children with Down syndrome. Sticky popsicle faces beaming in the sun, and twirling ballerinas with moon-eyed smiles. I felt as though I was the only person on the planet who felt the reality of carrying the living, kicking personification of devastation. I was angry, and I was bitter.

Harder still, I was faced with what it meant about me. Because the day that I met my beautiful little girl face to face, a bundle of pink, I knew the truth. My heartache had nothing to do with her. It wasn't rooted in her identity, but rather, in my understanding and knowledge of the world. A decade before, while studying to be a social worker, I'd learned the importance of examining bias; the active work of dismantling what you've been taught by life experience and society in order to grow and learn from something new. As a white, middle-class, educated woman, there was plenty of opportunity for practice in my career. I'd spent the better part of my adult life working toward recognizing that bias in myself and trying to make active change.

But in a moment when I was faced with the reality of where my pain in Lucy's diagnosis came from, I realized that I'd forgotten all the things I learned in those lecture halls. I wasn't grieving my little girl. I was grieving the things society had taught me were important. I was grieving straight A's and the cheerleading squad. Wedding veils and happy meals. I was grieving late night mud masks and painting toenails while giggling over ice cream sundaes. I was grieving what my ableism told me was now impossible. And that realization changed everything. I was able to look at my beautiful baby girl with new understanding; a knowledge that while this world isn't built for her, that doesn't make her any less worthy. It doesn't take away from her personhood. It can't negate the dignity she deserves, or the value she adds. So I wrapped my new girl in pink. I placed delicate bows on her head, and learned to delight in the ways she surprised me. I rocked her to sleep in the dark, sometimes with tears streaming down my face, but always with a thankful heart that she's changed me.

I still grieve sometimes. I grieve when people use slurs, or when legislation is passed that will impact my girl. I grieve the struggle of IEP meetings and fighting for access to services. I grieve for babies who will live in orphanages across the world, simple because of their sweet sandal-gapped toes. But there is also celebration. I've found the sticky popsicle days, and they are worth every moment of the heartache. So if you're still in the darkness—I see you. I've felt the suffocation and weight of that despair. It lives inside of me, and I'll never forget the way that feels. But I can tell you with an ardent heart there is joy on the other side. There is blessing in knowing that beautiful things can be hard—but that doesn't make them any less beautiful.

Lucy and I are cheering you on.

Even parents who work in a professional setting with individuals with disabilities may struggle to come to terms with an unexpected diagnosis. Adding to that initial shock, there are sometimes health risks and additional diagnoses that add a nuanced dimension of confusion and grief to the mix.

More Than One Diagnosis

By Virginia Wear, Mom and Advocate in the Down syndrome community

At my 38-week ultrasound my husband and I learned that our baby had a rare, life-threatening heart issue, and 50% of babies with this specific heart issue also have Trisomy 21. About a week later, mighty warrior feet marched into our lives as we welcomed our firstborn son, James. James spent the first 43 days of his life in the NICU.

From the moment of birth, we would witness undoubtable strength in our beautiful baby. He came out fighting for his life. And as his parents we experienced the sacred privilege of fighting alongside him. We waited weeks for the genetic test results as the hospital lost his cord blood that was sent for the first genetic test. When we finally received the diagnosis of Trisomy 21, my mind could not fathom the words intellectual disability regarding my son. The implications of the diagnosis rippled through my entire body, but none reached deeper than the question jarring my heart: how would this news shape his world?

At four months old, James received lifesaving open-heart surgery from the world's number one-ranked cardiothoracic surgeon followed by a brutal hospital stay. We trudged through each day until we were able to bring our baby home for the rest of his recovery. The very day James was cleared for travel our family of three eagerly left for Orange Beach, Alabama. My husband and I felt battle weary from those early days and desperately needed rest. It was on a beach walk six months after James' birth I began to unpack the Trisomy 21 diagnosis. There was finally space to acknowledge that this diagnosis shattered many dreams. With the ocean beside me I began to grieve the loss in quiet waves.

As I walked further, I sensed I'd been invited to a new dream, an even better dream. With my cheeks wet from tearful surrender, my YES rang with quiet resolve. I said YES to an unknown path that at that time stirred tremendous fear in me. I said yes to what I now consider the greatest adventure of my life. Today my son is a loving, healthy, social, adventure-seeking, gorgeous, growing toddler. Trisomy 21 no longer stirs fear or sadness in me. The word disability doesn't hold the sting it once held. Today my life is more joy filled than I could have ever imagined. In fact, my life is quite wonderful. I'm immensely thankful for my son and the incredible gift of his journey. And if given the chance, I would say a wholehearted yes to this path all over again.

Whether receiving a prenatal or birth diagnosis of Down syndrome for your child, your feelings are real and valid. None of your emotions are wrong and, as Elizabeth explained in detail earlier, there is a grief that is taking place. But the grief is not the end. The journey doesn't stop there. As I described at the beginning of the book, what I thought was the end of my life as I knew it, was only the beginning of a new chapter. So many find endless joy and boundless opportunities to share and spread joy.

Paving a Better Path for the Future

By Danielle Grandholm, Founder of Rising Kites

In May 2020, we welcomed our daughter, Sammie, into the world. Prior to her arrival, we had no indication that she would be born with Down syndrome or a number of health concerns. In a matter of minutes after her arrival, we went from believing we would be taking home a healthy, typically developing baby to learning our newborn had a genetic condition and some alarming health concerns. It was painful to hear, painful to process, and painful to accept. What should have been a joy-filled

(*continued*)

time became overshadowed by an overwhelming number of questions and fears. Though we were surrounded by caring and encouraging doctors, nurses, and staff, we were sent home with minimal resources—a printed-out paper defining "Down syndrome"—and nearly no indication of what to do next. The questions started pouring in.

- What do we do now?
- Who do we call?
- What does life look like from here?
- Is Sammie going to be okay?

Eventually, we found our footing. We connected with other families, established avenues of care for Sammie, and began to shift from fear to hope. But it became clear that our experience was not unique. So many other families were receiving a diagnosis with the same questions and the same ache. And many healthcare providers, despite their best intentions, felt ill-equipped to guide them.

Today, Rising Kites, a nonprofit celebrating the gift of Down syndrome, partners with medical providers, supports families from day one, and creates opportunities for individuals with Down syndrome to thrive and shine in their own unique ways.

A Little Extra

No matter the scenario you are facing or have already faced, there is an army of people who have gone before you. Many in this tribe are ready and willing to connect and share. It's a club you never knew you wanted to be a part of but once you are "in" you are accepted and loved. The diagnosis can feel isolating and lonely because people aren't often exposed to these communities until they are launched into them.

Even those who HAVE been around individuals with disabilities, like Amanda who has a Masters in Social Work, tend to feel like a fish out of water when a diagnosis knocks on their front door. The world you once knew changes shape and that can be very traumatic for many individuals. For some this is a big "T" Trauma and for others this is a little "t" Trauma. I have spoken to countless families who chose to receive counseling early on to unpack the emotions and feelings they've encountered from this unexpected twist.

Regardless of when and how you choose to process, I think all families would benefit from taking the time to grieve the dream that was lost and accept the path that was given. It can help clear out the wreckage to leave space for growth, renewal, acceptance, and a chance to thrive in your new reality.

CHAPTER 4

We're Home! Now What?

"Bit by bit, putting it together."

—Stephen Sondheim

Most parents feel a sense of excitement and fear when they walk out of the hospital with their newborn baby. The fragility of the situation can look and feel almost comical. Picture a husband and wife trying to put their tiny, newborn baby into a car seat that looks gigantic, for the first time. Once they finally figure out how to do that, they have to DRIVE with the most precious cargo they've ever carried. They drive slowly and cautiously on the highway to avoid any bumps or potential danger.

Once they've arrived safely home, there's a host of other "firsts" that come and the learning curve of feeding, sleeping, and general survival (both for the parent and child) can be steep. This feeling can be compounded by the added unknowns and fears that parents in the Down syndrome community face. Questions and concerns can race through your mind:

- Was it too soon to be discharged?
- Is the baby sleeping too much?
- Do I contact early intervention or does early intervention contact me?
- How will I know if my baby needs to go back to the hospital?

- Should I keep our current pediatrician or look for one that has more experience with children with Down syndrome?
- How do I find the right specialist for x,y,z?
- What if the hole in his heart has gotten bigger?
- What about feeding?

These are just a few of the worries expressed from parents who reach out to me through Happiness is Down syndrome. When Jed was in the NICU for seven days with an infection after birth, I worried he wouldn't come home soon, on the one hand, and wondered if he SHOULDN'T come home soon, on the other. It was an emotional, physical, spiritual roller coaster.

This chapter covers a few factors to consider for your child with Down syndrome coming home from the hospital, namely hypotonia, sleep and feeding.

Hypotonia

Eighty percent of babies with Down syndrome have *hypotonia*, or "low muscle tone" at birth. Since most newborns are fragile at birth, it can be difficult to understand how much hypotonia impacts infants with Down syndrome until you've held a baby with Down syndrome. Parents often describe a "wet noodle" feeling which can be intimidating, particularly for first-time parents.

In an article by Very Well Health entitled "Down syndrome: Symptoms and Intellectual and Physical Traits" Kathleen Fergus writes,

> "People with Down syndrome sometimes move awkwardly, usually due to low muscle tone (hypotonia) at birth which can interfere with physical development. Hypotonia often causes babies with Down syndrome to appear "floppy." The poor muscle tone can and often does improve with age and physical therapy. Still, most children with Down syndrome typically reach developmental milestones—sitting up, crawling, and walking—later than other kids. Low muscle tone may contribute to feeding problems and motor delays. Toddlers and older kids may have delays in speech and learning skills such as feeding, dressing, and toilet training."[1]

On Jed's first day of therapy, EVER, at just six weeks old, I was completely overwhelmed by all the things I didn't understand. To begin with, I didn't quite grasp why Jed needed physical therapy and what it would do for his low muscle tone. I remember his physical therapist, Kellie Janes, PT, DPT, PCS, patiently explaining hypotonia to me like this:

> "Imagine a rubber band. If the rubber band is brand new, it is taut and will snap back to its original shape and firmness quickly and easily. But if the rubber band has been stretched out a ton, it's going to be harder to conform back to what it was. Jed, with hypotonia, resembles the stretched out rubber band and it requires more effort for him to accomplish things."

Seeing that I wasn't quite getting it, she described something else:

> "Picture two branches of a tree. One is short and thick and the other is long and lean. The long and lean tree branch could sway easily in the breeze but it would take a much larger force to move or knock over the short, thick one. In terms of postural control, the long branch would need so much extra force to maintain stability in a storm. That is what it is like for many individuals with hypotonia."

This is crucial to understand early in our journey so (a) we can understand why physical therapy is necessary and beneficial from infancy and (b) we can remind ourselves not to be discouraged as parents when seemingly simple milestones take longer (sitting up, crawling, walking, etc.). Children and adults with Down syndrome can achieve the same milestones as anyone else but it often takes longer to master them. When we know that, we can support each individual with patience and care.

And while we're on the subject of patience, we should explore an area that weighs on the hearts and minds of any parent . . .

Sleep

When I became a mom for the first time, not only was I terrified of doing everything wrong, I was consumed with anything having to do with sleep (mostly because I wasn't getting any!). I immersed myself with books and resources to help sleep train my baby. It was a struggle and I don't think I've ever fully recovered from the exhaustion of those newborn days. When I learned that Jed, my second child, would have Down syndrome, I feared that there would be an entirely new and different learning curve. Yet again, I felt like I was facing a whole new world.

In 2019, the Down syndrome Association of Greater Charlotte shared,

> "Quality sleep is particularly hard to achieve for children with Down syndrome, where symptoms often persist into adulthood. According to the National Institute of Health, 76% of children with Down syndrome experience difficulty with the onset of sleep, their quality of REM sleep, and their ability to stay asleep. The sleep troubles children with Down syndrome face often affect other aspects of their development down the road."[2]

Experts in this field have discovered that sleep in early childhood, particularly infancy, can negatively impact learning, memory and language development. Research conducted by Jaime Edgin, PhD, has proven that to be true for children with Down syndrome, as well. Sleep interruptions and deprivation can be caused by a variety of factors and it's best to consult with your doctor first to discuss what is going on with your child. Two common causes of sleep disturbances in children with Down syndrome are *physical, breathing-related sleep problems* and *behavioral sleep problems.*

The Down Syndrome Association of the UK reports,

> "We know that around 50% of children who have Down's syndrome experience sleep issues. These may be behavioral in nature or have a physical cause such as obstructive sleep apnoea. This is where a person's normal breathing is disrupted during sleep because the walls of the throat relax and narrow or block the airway. Some children may have a complex mixture of behavioral and physical sleep problems. Bed time routines, consistent bedtime and waking times, going to

bed when tired, falling asleep without parents and avoiding excitement near bedtime are some of the things that help to lessen the likelihood of behavioral sleep problems."[3]

Many families who have children with Down syndrome just embarking on the journey have shared with me that their newborn babies sleep well and for longer durations than their typical children did (or do). This was definitely the case for us. In the first eight weeks of Jed's life, I would have to set an alarm to feed him every few hours because he would sleep well past the time he was supposed to eat.

This was a gift to me, on the one hand, because I was emotionally and physically exhausted from what I had endured during my pregnancy, birth, and the NICU experience. On the other hand, it was scary because Jed desperately needed to gain weight. We had to monitor his breastmilk and formula intake closely. So, when I let him sleep through his feeding times, I ran the risk of him not getting quite the amount he needed.

Feeding

Often, but not always, babies and toddlers with Down syndrome can experience difficulty with a bottle or breastfeeding and the journey moving to solid foods. Having the help of a pediatric speech pathologist or a board-certified lactation consultant can make all the difference in those early days, weeks, and months. But don't take my word for it.

From Breastfeeding to Solids: Tips from a Feeding Therapist

By Jill Rabin M.S. CCC-SLP/L IBCLC, Pediatric Speech Pathologist, Feeding Therapist, and International Board-Certified Lactation Consultant

My name is Jill Rabin, and I am a pediatric speech pathologist, feeding therapist, and international board-certified lactation

(*continued*)

consultant. I specialize in working with the 0–3 population and I frequently combine both of my professions together to assist pregnant, pumping and breastfeeding moms of babies with Down syndrome. I co-moderate a monthly free group through Julia's Way and the Massachusetts Down Syndrome Congress, helping coach mothers nationally and internationally on how to be successful in breastfeeding their baby with Down syndrome. Our goal has been to provide proper education and support to families with babies with Down syndrome who are interested in breastfeeding and/or providing breast milk to their baby.

I am frequently told by families that they were discouraged from breastfeeding by medical professionals, whether it be nurses, physicians, or therapists. This is especially true when there is a complex medical history such as prematurity, duodenal atresia, or a congenital heart defect. The focus is often on bottle-feeding and weight gain, especially if the baby is in the NICU. Direct breastfeeding is often not a priority.

A common thing that happens with babies with Down syndrome is that due to medical complexities, low tone, sleepiness, and poor endurance, breastfeeding often gets off to a slow start. It takes them longer to transition to exclusive breastfeeding. Moms may need to pump for an extended period and do a combination of breast and bottle. Many moms believe that if the baby doesn't transition to the breast within the first few weeks post birth, that it is not going to happen. This could not be farther from the truth. What I have found is that with time and the correct lactation support, while protecting the moms milk supply with pumping, not only do many of these babies transition to exclusive breastfeeding, but they often go on to breastfeed through toddlerhood. It should be noted that some babies with Down syndrome may transition right to the breast without difficulty just like their neurotypical peers.

The importance of breast milk for a baby with Down syndrome cannot be underestimated. It provides immunological and gut protective benefits, is easily digested and adapts to the baby's unique needs over time. It can also reduce the risk of obesity and can potentially lower the rates of celiac disease. While it is no secret that breast milk provides a multitude of healthful and immunological benefits for babies, the impact of the actual physical act of breastfeeding cannot be overlooked. Direct breastfeeding for an extended period, can help shape the hard palate, creating more of a "U" shape, resulting in a more patent airway and helping to allow for more space for teeth to descend without crowding. The deep jaw excursions that occur with breastfeeding can help with jaw strength and growth potentially helping in the development of the baby's airway. This can possibly help with prevention of sleep disordered breathing which is prevalent in the Down syndrome population. Breastfeeding also serves as oral motor exercise, strengthening the lips, tongue, and jaw.

Prenatal Preparation for Breastfeeding:

> If you have a prenatal diagnosis of Down syndrome and you know that you want to breastfeed your baby, there are many things that you can do to prepare for breastfeeding long before the baby is born. It is important to secure a breast pump in case you may need to pump after the baby is born, find an international board-certified lactation consultant that can guide you, take a breastfeeding class, and consider harvesting your colostrum toward the end of your pregnancy with your medical team's permission. Prenatal preparation helps you to be ready and gives you the power to advocate for breastfeeding and educate your medical team. There is a helpful blog post from Julia's Way that can help you prepare for breastfeeding journey in pregnancy.[4]

(*continued*)

Breastfeeding Your Baby with Down Syndrome in the First Few Hours:

> As we don't know what your baby's medical condition will be post-delivery, if they will need immediate medical care and if they won't be able to latch onto the breast right away, it is important to remember that you may need to start hand expression and pumping with an electric pump within the first six hours post-delivery. Frequent stimulation and emptying of the breasts can help you establish a strong milk supply so you can be prepared once the baby is medically ready. The key in the beginning is protecting your milk supply and requesting lactation support right away.

If your baby is medically stable right after delivery, you want to try to latch the baby on right after birth. This is referred to as the "golden hour." Babies who attach to the breast as their first exposure to feeding have something called "imprinting" that takes place and subsequent attempts at the breast will be easier. Babies with Down syndrome due to low tone can be sleepy and have poor endurance initially, and may not transfer milk well at the breast. They may initially require a combination of the bottle and breast until they are strong enough physically to transition to exclusive breastfeeding. Protection of your milk supply and qualitative practice at the breast with the help of an IBCLC are key. You may also need to use bridge devices like a nipple shield and supplemental nursing systems to help your baby at the breast temporarily until your baby is stronger. There is another Julia's Way blog post that can help in the first few hours after birth.[5]

Breastfeeding Your Baby with Down Syndrome Once You Get Home:

> It is very exciting once you can take your baby home with you, but the initial transition to exclusive breastfeeding

may take some time. Your baby may be excessively sleepy and not strong enough to transfer milk at the breast so again, protecting your milk with pumping and receiving support from an IBCLC are crucial. You may want to consider doing weighted feeds to monitor how much your baby can transfer from the breast, as it shows you progress and can provide a source of motivation when you see your baby transferring milk. In my experience, I have found that with babies with Down syndrome, it can take many of them 3–6 months in order to transition to the breast. Once they do make the transition, many of the babies go on to nurse through toddlerhood.

Just because your baby has Down syndrome does not mean that they can't breastfeed or receive human milk. Being educated about how to advocate for your baby, protect your milk supply and practice direct breastfeeding can contribute to your success. We need to continue to educate medical professionals about the health and oral structural benefits of breastfeeding babies with Down syndrome. Your baby can do this! For additional information, read the book "Breastfeeding and Down syndrome" edited by Ella Gray Cullen.[6]

In 2010 a colleague had returned back from a conference where Gill Rapley was one of the speakers. She handed me a video that was all about Gill Rapley's approach, which is called Baby-Led Weaning. Who knew that this 23-minute video would totally change my life as a feeding therapist?

In watching the video, I was amazed by watching these 6- to 12-month-old neurotypical babies self-feed different table foods. As I watched the video, I thought about my 0–3 patient caseload, and felt that this approach could be very therapeutic, especially for my patients with Down syndrome. I had to figure out how to do it safely as I knew they would require more support. That is how the Adapted Baby-Led Weaning Approach® was born!

(continued)

Over the years in working with babies with Down syndrome, I saw many of them struggle with solid foods. I would see two- and three-year-olds still being spoon fed by adults, refusing textured foods and not having any chewing skills. After viewing the video about Gill Rapley's approach, I started making changes in how I implemented feeding therapy with my patients with Down syndrome using baby-led principles. While ABLW follows all the same principles of traditional baby-led weaning, there are some things that are done differently.

First, from birth the baby with Down syndrome should be working with a physical therapist to establish core and strong gross motor foundational skills so they can be ready to sit up in a highchair when they are six months old. Secondly, we focus on prefeeding skill development from birth to six months, working on the jaw, lips, cheeks, and tongue with oral motor exercises, in preparation for the solid food transition. We also encourage hand-to-mouth skills for mouthing of hands, fingers and then toys. This helps with desensitizing the gag and sensory mapping of the mouth in preparation for eating.

Once solids are introduced, the size, shape and texture are used therapeutically to safely advance feeding skill development. Also, bridge devices such as a silicone feeder may need to be used to help with hand-to-mouth skills and to help refine chewing. A silicone feeder often has bifurcated handles making it easy for the baby to hold, and the top of the feeder has nipple-like structure that looks like a pacifier with holes in it that allows the food placed in it to come out in a mashed form. It is a great bridge device that can be used to safely work on chewing skills.

Many medical professionals may discourage you from doing a baby-led approach to solids with your baby with Down syndrome, but with adapted baby-led weaning, it can be done safely. If your baby with Down syndrome has a complex medical history, it may delay the onset of starting solid foods, but it is still possible. With adapted baby-led weaning, we are always targeting feeding skill development with use of differently sized and shaped table foods (food strips and partially exposed foods) and with bridge devices. With time, patience and the guidance of an experienced feeding therapist, babies with Down syndrome can absolutely do a baby-led weaning approach to solids. It results in great chewing skills; intuitive eating and the baby is eating the same whole and nutrient-dense foods as the rest of the family.

It certainly doesn't conclude with what Jill shared, above. In so many ways, the way a child with Down syndrome learns to eat, shapes their future health, and lays a foundation for the way they will move throughout their years. In my case, Jed was diagnosed in the early days with Laryngomalacia, which is a common birth defect in the larynx (voice box) that causes floppy tissue above the vocal cords to collapse into the airway during inhalation, leading to a noisy breathing sound called stridor. This impacted his feeding, his difficulty gaining weight, and caused acid reflux during the first six to eight months of his life. We learned that early detection of this is so helpful, combined with speech and feeding therapy. We found a feeding therapist at a nearby clinic who observed Jed while he was eating and helped him improve his posture and positioning while doing so. By having that weekly practice with Jedidiah, we noticed a vast improvement over time.

Let's hear more from an expert who breaks down how feeding and speech are connected and how they can contribute to lifelong, positive development and growth.

Oral Muscle Development Is the Key to Unlocking Speech Clarity and Feeding Development

By Heather Vukelich (SLP and Feeding Specialist)

As a speech and feeding therapist who is very passionate about serving the Down syndrome community, I realized early on that in order to make an impact in a child's speech clarity and feeding

(*continued*)

development that I would have to treat the oral and facial muscles. It was a very pivotal day in my early career when I was involved in a barbecue lunch at our local Down syndrome organization (shout out to the DSCBA!). As I watched each child use their tongue to mash food against the roof of their mouth, I realized a couple of things. First, that many children with Down syndrome were unable to chew food properly, which severely limited nutritional intake and put them at higher risk for constipation, choking, and aspiration.

Secondly, if one muscle group is overactive (tongue), then the others must be under-active (jaw, lips, cheeks). This muscle imbalance was reflected directly into straw and cup drinking as well. Children often wrapped their tongue around a straw or cup instead of using their lips and cheeks to draw liquid. Very quickly I came to realize the relationship between feeding and speech clarity development. This is because the same muscles are used for both functions. As children grow through their first year, their oral motor development translates directly into how prepared they are for speech sound development. In this example the child who has overused his tongue for feeding and drinking will overuse his tongue when developing speech. Furthermore he may lack oral-sensory connection with the jaw, lips and cheeks, making sound development disordered and the ability to imitate speech sounds/words extremely difficult. Not only does this cause issues in specific speech sound development, but also in the growth of the overall oral-facial complex.

The balance of facial muscle pressures contributes to the oral-facial growth. A balanced system ensures the forward growth of the upper and lower mandibles, which determines proper airway development. It's been an ongoing educational journey connecting with a team of providers to holistically facilitate the growth and development of my client's oral-facial complex. A good team includes an airway-focused orthodontist, dentist, and ENT. I find this team approach yields the best results in the overall development of a child's feeding, speech clarity, and airway.

The other overarching lesson I've learned over the years is to NEVER, EVER LOSE HOPE. One of my biggest accomplishments and strongest memories was helping an 18-year-old woman improve her speech clarity and confidence in a matter of five years. I knew this was possible because I had strong mentors who taught me that muscles have the ability to change at any time. This reality gives me unlimited hope and our children unlimited potential independent of their age. I've experienced it time and time again as children develop throughout their lives, that each age and stage opens the door to opportunities for growth and success. Hope-filled oral-sensory motor education is a necessary component to helping families through the speech clarity and feeding journey. These journeys can often take time to achieve. We must remember that parents are the strongest factor in a child's success. This constantly encourages me to create positive family-centered therapeutic opportunities, courses and offerings.

A Little Extra

In the early days, it is common to feel overwhelmed. When Jed was a baby, I learned firsthand about appointment fatigue, which refers to feeling mentally and physically drained after attending a series of appointments, particularly when they are back-to-back or lengthy. It can be a lot to take in, so it is important to make sure you aren't inundating yourself with too much. It helped me to wake up each day and ask, "What is *one* thing I can do for my child with Down syndrome today and *one* thing I can do for myself today." Reach out to local and online community chats when you just need to connect with another parent who understands the overwhelm. *You are not alone.*

CHAPTER 5

Abbreviations and Learning Curves and Therapies, Oh My!

"If you can't fly, then run. If you can't run, then walk. If you can't walk, then crawl. But, whatever you do, you have to keep moving forward."

—Martin Luther King Jr.

OT, PT, DI, SLP, IFSP, EI. . .

These abbreviations and so many more flopped around in my head, like a fish pulled out of water, looking for a place to land for the days, weeks and months following Jed's birth.

Upon entering the Down syndrome community, I didn't know what anything meant. I would walk into a doctor's office or meet with a therapist and hear terminology I'd never heard before which made me feel like I was somehow failing as Jed's mom. I felt a twinge of guilt and shame when I had to ask, "What is that?" Or, "Can you please explain what you mean by that?" I constantly felt like I needed to be an instant expert in things I had never even heard of before.

On the morning of Day 3 of Jed being in the NICU, I found it impossible to get out of bed. The pain of my C-section was all encompassing and the growing number of question marks in my brain had me completely paralyzed. I desperately wanted to be with my baby in the hospital, but every time I would start to rise out of bed, I would instantly sink back down with fear, confusion, and a deep sense of overwhelm. I harkened back to the old adage I'd learned from the song in *FROZEN II* and decided to do the next right thing. I called ONE number I'd been given and spoke to a case worker who helped me understand the process of Early Intervention (abbreviated, "EI"—hooray, one down, 10 million to go!). That man was a Godsend and, though I cannot remember his name, I will always be thankful for his guidance to me on that hot summer morning as I lay, buried beneath my sheets for shelter.

Through this brief conversation I gathered a few helpful pieces of information that I've carried with me in my toolbox:

- Every county is different when it comes to Early Intervention (EI).
- Every U.S. state and territory offers early intervention services.
- For children from birth to three years old, you can contact your state's early intervention service for information on how to receive services.
- For children three years or older, you should contact your local elementary school or school district to request an evaluation. Before we look into the other concerns of bringing your baby home from the hospital, let's explore Early Intervention.

Armed with the basics after that phone call, I was able to get myself out of bed. Too many abbreviations and facts can muddle the mind but small snippets of useful information for the present moment feels empowering! Once Jed came home from the hospital, we quickly moved down the path to Early Intervention.

In the weeks that followed, Jedidiah began receiving his services through a computer screen, during the COVID-19 lockdown (what a time!). Early Intervention services kicked in quickly and, until his third birthday, we had Physical Therapy (PT) Speech Therapy with an SLP (Speech and Language Pathologist), Occupational Therapy (OT), and Developmental Intervention (DI) coming to our house to work with him once or twice a week.

Those abbreviations that were a total mystery to me in the beginning, became more clear as we met each therapist, one by one. We found this period of time to be very helpful for him and for us, as his caregivers. Through the guidance and direction of the professionals entering our home, we felt like we had "on-the-job" training about how to best support Jed.

Before the brief overview I received over the phone and the real-time experience of Early Intervention, I didn't have a clue as to why we needed it, nor how it would benefit my son. Having a clear explanation laid out for me beforehand would have been invaluable in grasping what we were doing. In keeping with that, here's a comprehensive explanation to get us started!

The Importance of Early Intervention

By Masina Dua, M.S. CCC-SLP, Speech-Language Specialist

Early intervention programs can provide support and services for infants and toddlers with developmental delays and disabilities. These services will depend on the needs of your child. They can include speech therapy, physical therapy, and more. Every U.S. state and territory offers early intervention services.

Early intervention services are custom made to the specific needs of every child and family and are outlined in an individualized Family Service Plan (IFSP). Services are typically provided in familiar settings like the home or daycare, where children naturally participate. Early intervention recognizes the crucial role of families and provides support to empower them to meet their child's needs.

Early intervention can significantly impact a child's development, potentially leading to better outcomes in the long run. When you face head-on certain delays in the early days, it can be more cost-effective and impactful in the long run than waiting until delays become more pronounced. Waiting until a child with Down syndrome is older will often require more intensive

(*continued*)

interventions. Early intervention can also provide family support and resources, helping them to better understand and meet their child's needs.

The first years of life are a critical time in a child's development. Research consistently shows that early intervention services provided to infants and toddlers can significantly improve overall developmental outcomes and family well-being. These services, especially when delivered through a family-centered model, empower parents to become active, confident participants in supporting their child's unique needs.

The benefits of early diagnostics and services are profound and evidence-based. When we intervene early, we not only support the child, we also build competency and confidence in caregivers, creating a ripple effect that strengthens the entire family system. It is during this window of early development, when the brain is incredibly adaptable, that we can most positively influence a child's growth. Early intervention addresses all domains of development: cognitive, adaptive, motor, communication, and social-emotional. In the Down syndrome community, the presentation of needs is wide-ranging. The extra copy of chromosome 21 affects both brain and body development, resulting in individualized profiles that may include physical, cognitive, and behavioral differences. While some children may experience only mild delays, others may require more extensive support.

It's important to emphasize at this point, that the needs of each child will often differ greatly. One child with Down syndrome may qualify for Occupational Therapy, while another does not. Some children will qualify for Physical Therapy several times a week because of their specific physical needs while another only receives it a couple of times a month. The services should be catered to each individual case.

When I was a new parent to a child with a disability, I lacked the ability to identify what Jed needed and didn't need. Particularly when it came to fine and gross motor skills. Having a skilled therapist in my home opened my eyes to the little things Jed was having a hard time grasping (literally and figuratively) that I might have otherwise missed.

Occupational Therapy at a Glance

By Caitlin Rossettini, MOT, OTR/L

Occupational therapy services focus on a person's daily occupations. For children with Down syndrome this may include motor development (including both fine and gross motor), self-care skills, feeding skills, self-regulation, sensory processing, and play skills.

A child with Down syndrome may face challenges in these areas due to developmental delays or physiological differences, including low muscle tone or relatively short limbs. Through occupational therapy a child with Down syndrome can achieve crucial developmental milestones, increase their independence in their daily routines, engage independently in school activities, and participate in play with peers. A child's main occupation, and crucial part of development, is to engage in play. Imagine a playground—you may see children playing tag, climbing up the stairs to go down the slide or play pirates up top, or in the sand pit digging for treasure.

Children with Down syndrome may have trouble running or climbing due to decreased overall strength, challenges with motor planning, or impaired balance. They may not feel safe on a playground structure because they are not sure where their body is in space with sensory processing difficulties. In a sandbox, using the appropriate amount of force to dig or manipulate tools can present challenges. These are just a few things a child with Down syndrome may encounter on the playground alone, ones that should be easy and fun for most kids.

Occupational therapy from birth to preschool age is mostly rooted in play-based and child-centered therapy. Skilled and targeted therapy can help a child access their environment,

(*continued*)

participate in daily routines, and engage in play. These skills can profoundly impact how a child engages with peers and participation in family activities. Providing a child the opportunity to meaningfully engage in what is most important to them and their family is the ultimate goal of a pediatric occupational therapist. Though a skill may be difficult or take a longer time to acquire, all the smiles, giggles, and pride in every small win make it a wonderfully fulfilling experience.

Each child enrolled in pediatric occupational therapy will have their own individualized goals to meet their needs after a full evaluation. And, like every other discipline, each child will have different strengths and weaknesses to work with. I remember a time in Jed's development when it seemed he might not ever be able to grip a spoon or fork to eat his food or apply enough pressure to snap a lid closed. Those things came along the more we incorporated applicable actions and encouraged Jed to get involved in things around the house (sweeping/holding a dustpan, helping wash the dishes, emptying and filling the laundry bin, practicing folding the clothes OUT of the laundry bin, etc.). It's really exciting and fun to watch this branch of therapy come alive in tasks around the house. It's also another fantastic way to connect and bond with your child!

That desire to bond with my son has been there since the moment I felt him kick inside my belly. It feels silly to say it now because of my amazingly strong connection to Jed but, in those initial diagnosis days, I wondered if he would be able to speak. I had such little knowledge of the capacity of an individual with Down syndrome and held on to the small point of reference I had through watching the actor who played Corky in the show in the 1990s called, "Life Goes On." He spoke relatively clearly. Would my Jed be able to communicate as effectively? Would we be able to have a close bond through conversation? I've heard this concern echoed from countless parents. Let's unpack some of the specifics.

The ABCs of Speech

By Masina Dua, M.S. CCC-SLP (Speech-Language Specialist)

Speech and language are two areas of development that have a high likelihood of being impacted for children born with Down syndrome. It is important to understand the distinction between Speech and Language.

- Speech is motoric; it is the act of precisely coordinating muscles, airflow, and articulators (tongue, lips, jaw, etc.) to formulate sound and syllable combinations, in order to create words, and be able to combine those words into longer strings of complex utterances, which becomes connected-spoken-speech. Simply put, Speech is motor planning, articulation, voice, and fluency.
- Language is how we understand the world and communicate our ideas in a meaningful, effective way; it is our vocabulary, grammar, syntax, semantics, and communication in social contexts (pragmatics).

Children with Down syndrome may face challenges in developing clear and functional speech due to the presence of physiological differences. Dr. Dawn Ewing, executive director of the International Academy of Biological Dentistry and Medicine said, "From clinical awareness and scientific study, we know that what happens in the mouth is reflected in the body, and what happens in the body is reflected in the mouth."

Hypotonia is a common characteristic of Down syndrome that both children and adults can experience; it is characterized by reduced muscle tone, which can impact an individual's gross and fine motor development, as well as their ability to coordinate their body. Hypotonia can affect a range of areas critical to speech development, such as sitting posture, core strength, breath support, oral muscle tone, and the coordination required for precise speech movements.

(*continued*)

Low tone can affect oral positioning at rest; rather than having "lips closed, while breathing through the nose," individuals with Down syndrome may present with an open mouth posture, forward tongue placement, and/or oral breathing. Airway management and intervention to facilitate a closed-mouth posture is especially important for these children who do consistently breathe through their mouths. Habitual mouth breathing has the potential to impact overall health by reducing oxygen absorption to the brain and body, dental issues, sleep disturbances, and can cause changes in facial structure.

Hypotonia in conjunction with craniofacial differences is common. Individuals with Down syndrome may present with a smaller palate and maxilla (upper jaw), which can reduce the size of the nasopharynx (the connection between the nose and the rest of the respiratory system), limiting the ability to breathe through their nose, and could also contribute to the open mouth posturing. Facial anatomy, upper airway differences, and a narrowed auditory canal can predispose individuals with Down syndrome to frequent ear infections and middle ear complications. These issues, along with difficulties in eating, drinking, swallowing, or hearing, have the potential to interfere with a child's ability to acquire speech and language.

With these factors in mind, early and targeted therapy plays a vital role. It supports safe and effective motor movements while strengthening the muscles and coordination of both the body and oral articulators, skills that are essential for clear speech and meaningful communication. Language development through speech therapy in the birth-to-three population is fundamentally play-based, rooted in relationship-building, and family-education. Children learn through play, and when that play is consistent, intentional, and tailored to their needs, it can be impactful to their development. Targeted therapy can improve breath support, strengthen oral musculature, encourage vocabulary development, and foster receptive and expressive language growth, all of which enrich a child's ability to connect with others.

When a child with Down syndrome, or any child for that matter, is empowered to express themselves, they build confidence, social awareness, and a sense of identity. While some children may experience mild impacts, others face what can feel like a perfect storm of challenges from day one. But early, consistent, individualized intervention and speech therapy can be a game-changer. It supports not just the mechanics of speech but the emotional, social, and relational aspects of communication, while connecting children with their caregivers, families, and the world. Early intervention can begin any time after birth; there is no such thing as "missing the boat," but the sooner it starts, the better.

Children with Down syndrome are more likely to experience a level of delay in motor, social, and speech-language development; some may also face intellectual disabilities, attention challenges, or working memory difficulties. Medical concerns (e.g., congenital heart defects, hearing loss, vision problems, gastrointestinal conditions, or thyroid issues) can be present from birth or emerge over time, adding layers of complexity that may feel overwhelming. Taking action early can offer caregivers a sense of agency and build clarity in a process that often feels unpredictable and uncontrollable. Starting a journey, any journey, requires preparation.

Before we embark, we fill the gas tank, pack snacks, and plan our route. Even when that plan changes (as it often does), having a foundation and a route to follow can give us comfort and the confidence to even go. The same is true for early intervention. When families have information, a roadmap, and a trusted team, they are better prepared to navigate the unknown. Early intervention helps families speak the same language, literally and figuratively. It empowers them to participate fully in their child's development, build stronger relationships, and create a supportive, informed environment to make decisions.

I was a Speech-Language Pathologist deeply experienced in the Early Intervention system long before I ever became a

(*continued*)

mother. But when my own newborn was experiencing significant and pervasive challenges and delays, I felt helpless. Despite thoroughly knowing the developmental markers, therapy, and procedure, my feelings overpowered me, and good-intentioned people told me to just "wait and see." My professional practice reflected the opposite of that, so I fearfully leaned into what I knew. I called specialists, booked appointments, and pursued a myriad of evaluations, while equally floating through my days like an anxiety-riddled zombie, and crying myself to sleep at night. On one side of me was the seasoned professional making clinical decisions; on the other, a terrified mother overwhelmed by guilt, uncertainty, and the unknown. Intervening early became the hand that guided even me, a person who conceptually "knew the route;" it helped me build a foundation not just for my child, but for my family, a foundation rooted in information, empowerment, love, resilience, and hope.

If I could offer one message to parents who are at any point of a journey with their child, who are unsure, afraid, or overwhelmed, it would be this, you do not need to have all the answers. You do not need to be fully ready. You do not need to wonder if it is too early, or be afraid that it is too late. You just need to take one step. Early intervention is not about judgment or pressure. It is about support. It is about giving your child, and yourself, the tools and community to grow with confidence; to know, no matter where you are on the road, you are not alone.

Throughout Jed's speech journey, there have been highs and lows. There have been moments where I truly thought he would be among the first of his peers to speak. By the time he turned five with very few words, I knew that my assessment had been incorrect. Sometimes it feels like three steps forward, two steps back. But I have seen time and time again that individuals with Down syndrome are resilient and capable. Jed does things on his own watch and that timing doesn't often match mine. When waves of discouragement come on this journey (which they inevitably will), I cling to the hope of knowing I am doing everything in my power to help him succeed, and he is in phenomenal hands with the instruction of his therapists. When the challenging times come, I have other parents to share with and professional advice to seek.

One particular area of struggle we've had is with potty training. Once again, I find myself looking back on times when I thought we would have this mastered, only to be forced back to the drawing board. Only recently, upon attending a webinar about potty training a child with Down syndrome, did I realize that my experience was completely normal in our community. It is par for the course that many families take two steps forward, three steps back. Finding specialists and support has been vital for me on this journey.

The Building Blocks of Potty Training

By Kimberly Yaeger, President and Founder of Little Leaf Learning Center

When it comes to potty training, starting as early as eighteen months—with a proven, gentle method—gives children with Down syndrome such a strong foundation for success. When families offer the chance to begin early, kids have the opportunity to be potty trained right alongside their typically developing peers. That simple shift can open the door to growth, confidence, and a new skill that bridges a social gap our little ones never needed to carry in the first place.

Children with Down syndrome have a physiology that's beautifully unique—shaped by that little something extra, the third copy of the 21st chromosome. Some of these differences we can see, but many are internal and easy to overlook. Hypotonia, extra-stretchy connective tissue, and differences in sensory processing aren't visible on the outside, yet they influence how children build strength, awareness, and coordination. As people with only two copies of that chromosome, we may never fully understand what these differences feel like from the inside, but we can keep in mind that they affect how quickly and comfortably our little ones learn skills like sitting, walking, talking, and of course—potty training.

(*continued*)

Potty training requires a blend of muscle strength, coordination, and something even more subtle: the shift from an unconscious awareness of bodily sensations to a conscious understanding of what those signals mean. Our children may simply need more time and support to make that transition. That's not a setback—it's just part of their natural developmental rhythm.

Potty training is so much more than a developmental milestone. It's a moment to recognize a child's abilities, their courage, and their desire to learn and grow. Children with Down syndrome absolutely deserve these early opportunities. And when we delay simply because we assume they aren't ready, we may unintentionally close a door they were perfectly capable of walking—or even crawling—through. Beginning early isn't about pressure or perfection—it's about trusting who they are right now and giving them the space to show what they can do.

And please remember, you never have to navigate this journey alone. There is support, guidance, and encouragement available every step of the way. With a little patience, a thoughtful plan, and steady reassurance, children truly can develop this skill in their own time. Starting early allows you to ease into the process gently and lovingly, exploring together and slowly building expectations that won't overwhelm your child. It also helps families avoid many of the challenging behaviors that often arise when potty training begins at three, four, or even later.

And the best part? This gentle method works beautifully no matter when you begin. While early opportunities are incredibly helpful, it is never too late to start potty training The Little Leaf Way: A Gentle Journey to Potty Training Children with Down Syndrome. Older children can thrive with the same supportive, respectful approach—gaining confidence, independence, and pride in their growing abilities. When we give children this chance, they so often surprise us in the most wonderful ways. Potty training becomes more than a skill on a checklist—it becomes a message of confidence and respect. It says, We see your potential. We believe in you. And we're walking this journey right beside you.

A Little Extra

Knowledge is power, and every therapist and specialist who works with your child has expert knowledge to share. I became like a sponge, soaking up all the understanding I could so I would have some awareness of what was going on with my child. I collected my notes from therapies and appointments, as well as pamphlets and assessments in a three ring binder so I could easily jar my memory between sessions. Each day became more empowering, because I began to feel like I was a part of something. As Kimberly mentioned, we do not have to walk this path alone.

Please remember that the early intervention therapists are there to help equip you and your child. It can be stressful, at times, to have people coming in and out of your house, especially on the heels of giving birth or coming home from the NICU. Give yourself grace and remember that your house doesn't need to be tidied or in order for these therapists. They've seen it all and many understand the complexity and newness of the situation you find yourself in.

CHAPTER 6

Myth vs. Reality

"We have the same wants and dreams as everyone else. We can do anything anyone else can do. We are more alike than we are different."

—Advocacy manager at the National Down Syndrome Society

As I shared in Chapter 1, up until my prenatal diagnosis, I had little to no exposure to the world of Down syndrome. Because of this, I reverted to the ideas I'd heard perpetuated in society. Thoughts of my son becoming a burden to those around him flew through my mind because I had not yet experienced the joy of having someone with Down syndrome in my life. I'm sad to admit that I second guessed the things he would be able to do because I hadn't seen anyone with Down syndrome do much of, well . . . anything . . . before. Exposure and inclusion is the name of the game when it comes to ripping down bias, ableism, and archaic notions. We'll cover this in more detail in Chapter 10.

Without a doubt, the hardest part about parenting a child with a disability, for me, is not my child and it's not even the disability. It's about the ancient and archaic borders and grandiose ideas built up around people with Down syndrome. It's about the extremes in two directions:

- **1st Extreme: Sainthood:** "He's an angel sent from heaven, and you are a saint picked by God to take care of this child for a holy purpose." While this sounds beautiful and is often very well intended, it puts both the child and the parents at a disadvantage by neglecting to acknowledge the human of the people. It puts them on a pedestal rather than getting the help and resources that are often needed. It puts us on an island when we really need to be in the middle of a community.
- **2nd Extreme: Pity and Ableism:** This is the extreme that denies the inherent worth, beauty, and value in a person with a disability. It makes the assumption that any life that falls outside the norm of society must be pitied at the very least or obliterated at the very worst. (We will discuss ableism more in depth in a later chapter.)

Disability is not the problem. The sooner we can come together on this fact as a society, the better off all of us will be. The fact remains, however, that there are currently many biases surrounding Down syndrome. Much of those preconceived notions are based in archaic ideas and outdated constructs that were pervasive in the mid to late 1900s. There was (and is) so much to learn about Trisomy 21 and the journey is fluid. Science is constantly revealing new pieces to the puzzle and brilliant minds in our community are continuously helping to uncover the possibilities with individuals with Down syndrome.

People don't know what they don't know and, even I, before Jed was born, often assumed many of the myths listed next were true.

Myth: It's called "*Downs* syndrome."

Reality: It's called Down syndrome after John Langdon Down. The "Down" is not plural and it's not referring to the temperament of individuals with Down syndrome. I regularly hear people say, "I call it UP syndrome because individuals with Down syndrome aren't 'Down' they are 'Up.' This often takes on a playful tone and, in the next chapter, you will hear a sibling describe his brother as 'Up,' not

'Down.'" It's pretty common. The most important facts to remember with this are, (1) The syndrome is named after a man's last name—"Down" and (2) Individuals with Down syndrome are not always upbeat. To believe so can perpetuate another myth, which is . . .

Myth: Individuals with Down syndrome are always happy.

Reality: People with Down syndrome experience the full gamut of emotion just like any other human being. To always classify them as "happy" is to dehumanize them and generalize. This myth is among the most common because many individuals with Down syndrome are quite lovely to be around. There is a reason many of the statistics about being happy with their lives exist. But this does not mean that all people with Down syndrome feel this way, act this way, or ARE this way. Every person on this planet carries unique characteristics of their own and cannot be broadly defined.

Myth: There is a spectrum when it comes to Down syndrome.

Reality: Down syndrome is not a spectrum disorder. It is a genetic condition caused by the presence of an extra copy of the 21st chromosome. A person is born with Down syndrome or they aren't and no one has a more or less severe version. Some individuals with Down syndrome may have advanced reading, math, communication, or physical skills than others, but that's not because their Down syndrome is "less severe." As with typical individuals, everyone has different strengths and weaknesses. With the different types of Down syndrome—Trisomy 21, translocation Down syndrome, and mosaic Down syndrome—each has its own unique characteristics and may present with different symptoms and challenges. However, all individuals with Down syndrome share the same underlying genetic cause—the presence of an extra chromosome 21.

Myth: All individuals with Down syndrome have health problems.

Reality: As with any individual, there can be a variety of health challenges. Individuals with Down syndrome are often at risk for more health challenges than their typical peers but the assumption cannot be made that all people with Down syndrome are sick or suffering. With the progress of modern science and medicine, many conditions or health concerns that were once catastrophic are now manageable or treatable. For instance, lifesaving heart surgery is now commonplace for the 50% of individuals born with a heart defect.

Myth: Only older parents have children with Down syndrome.

Reality: According to Centers for Disease Control and Prevention research, about 80% of children who have Down syndrome are born to women younger than 35. The CDC research shows that the chance of having a baby with Down syndrome does increase with age. However, younger women have more babies, so more children with Down syndrome are born to younger mothers.

Myth: A child born with Down syndrome will cause the demise of a marriage.

Reality: The Vanderbilt Kennedy Study published in the *American Association of Intellectual Disabilities* showed that divorce rates are *lower* in families of children with Down syndrome. This was one of the largest studies to date and included 647 families who have children with Down syndrome.[1] This is not to downplay the challenges that can come with having a child with a disability, particularly those with medical complications. However, if you speak to families in the Down syndrome community, you will often hear stories of love and connection that are enhanced by their loved one with a disability.

Myth: Down syndrome is a rare disorder.

Reality: Down syndrome is the most commonly occurring chromosomal condition.[2] Approximately 1 in every 770 babies in the United States is born with Down syndrome, or around 5,000 births per year.

Myth: Down syndrome is hereditary and runs in families.

Reality: Translocation, a type of Down syndrome that accounts for 3–4% of all cases, is the only type of Down syndrome known to have a hereditary component. Of those, one-third (or 1% of all cases of Down syndrome) are hereditary.

Myth: All people with Down syndrome have a severe cognitive disability.

Reality: Most people with Down syndrome have a mild to moderate cognitive disability, or intellectual disability. This is not indicative of the many strengths and talents that each individual possesses. It's important to keep an open mind and treat each person with dignity, respect, patience, and kindness.

Myth: We already know all there is to know about Down syndrome.

Reality: Though we know that an extra full or partial copy of chromosome 21 causes the characteristics of Down syndrome, researchers are making great strides in identifying how individual genes on chromosome 21 affect a person with Down syndrome. Scientists now feel strongly that it will be possible to improve, correct, or prevent many of the health problems associated with Down syndrome in the future.

Myth: A child with Down syndrome negatively impacts their sibling.

Reality: As I shared with my sons, recent studies also support the fact that a child with Down syndrome will usually not have a negative impact on siblings. For example, a recent study published in the *Journal of Intellectual Disability Research* found no long-term detrimental effects to siblings. In fact, some mental health professionals point to the psychological advantages of such a child cared for within the family circle. They have documented siblings who have increased tolerance, compassion, and awareness, in contrast to all typical siblings.

Myth: People who have Down syndrome die young.

Reality: The average life expectancy for a person with Down syndrome is nearly 60 years old. Some people with Down syndrome have lived into their 80s. It is true that people with Down syndrome on average don't live as long as their typical counterparts. And, unfortunately, the average life expectancy for the black Down syndrome community in the United States is just 35 years old. This is obviously concerning and deserves intensified time and attention.

Myth: People who have Down syndrome cannot walk or play sports.

Reality: Most individuals with Down syndrome can and DO walk. Early intervention plays a vital role in providing physical therapy to lay the groundwork for proper form and can help move along a propensity for sports. Individuals with Down syndrome have a variety of athletic abilities, interests, and levels of agility, in the same way neurotypical individuals do. Getting involved in programs like the Special Olympics or GiGi Fit can help foster and improve physicality and get the body moving and strengthened.

Myth: People with Down syndrome can't read or write.

Reality: The majority of children with Down syndrome can learn to read and write. The most effective way to teach reading to children with disabilities, including children with Down syndrome, is by using teachers who are well trained with high expectations of their students, and students' progress is formally evaluated. More research is needed to determine how to most effectively teach children with Down syndrome to read and write.

Myth: People with Down syndrome all look alike.

Reality: Many but not all people with Down syndrome share common features. For example, many but not all people with Down syndrome have almond-shaped eyes and a short stature. However, like typical people who share similar features, they often look more like their families than each other.

Myth: Adults who have Down syndrome cannot live independently or get jobs.

Reality: An increasing number of adults with Down syndrome in the United States are living independently with limited assistance from family members or the state. A small percentage are able to live entirely independently. In the United States, some students who have Down syndrome graduate from high school, and some go on to attend post-secondary education. More opportunities are available for education and employment today than ever before. Anecdotally, we know that people with Down syndrome can be excellent employees and some employers have reported a higher satisfaction level among ALL workers when they have co-workers who have Down syndrome.

The longer I exist in this community, the more I realize we've only scratched the surface of what growth looks like in the lives of individuals with Down syndrome. There is limitless potential, particularly with many of the existing and up-and-coming services and programs available. Be sure to read the self-advocate chapter to meet some individuals with Down syndrome living their best lives.

A Little Extra

Why does it matter to myth-bust? Because opportunities can only evolve and exist when we are operating in truth and knowledge. If society isn't properly informed about individuals with Down syndrome, assumptions arise about whether or not they can or should participate in society. There should be a collective desire for inclusion, opportunity, and promotion of those who are different and uniquely fashioned. That's what this community is all about. We can embrace every opportunity to share from a place of humility and love when these myths are being spread and perpetuated.

CHAPTER 7

The Sanctity of Sibling Relationships

"A child is like a butterfly in the wind. Some can fly higher than others, but each one flies the best it can. Why compare one against the other? Each one is different. Each one is special. Each one is beautiful."

—Anonymous

"What about my older son? How will having a sibling with Down syndrome impact Clay?"

This question blared loudly in my mind after receiving that fateful phone call from my OB in March 2020. I was worried about a variety of potential scenarios in those initial moments and was unable to think clearly. Luckily the guidance of our genetic counselor just a few days later was timely and helpful. She pointed to various studies showing that siblings of individuals with Down syndrome often experience a unique blend of challenges and positive growth. While some may experience increased responsibility or anxiety, the 2011 study by Brian Skotko and Susan P. Levine[1] indicated the following:

- More than 96% said they loved their sibling with Down syndrome.

- 94% of older siblings said they were proud of their loved one with Down syndrome, and 88% also said they were better people because of their sibling.
- More than 90% planned to remain involved in their sibling's life as they grew older.

When we brought Jed home from the NICU, our then 2 ½-year-old little boy, Clay, ran down the stairs from his nap and peered into the bassinet in the corner where sweet little 5-pound, 8-oz Jed was sleeping soundly. A smile broke out across his face bigger than I had ever seen before. He was instantly enamored by his brother and wanted to hold him, caress him, giggle with him, sing to him, and talk to him. For our family, the connection was instantaneous and glorious. Many siblings I've encountered in the Down syndrome community have expressed similar feelings of connection and gratitude for their brother or sister.

In addition, there can also be a feeling of responsibility that develops, long before any sort of caregiving duties are entrusted to them. For instance, the other night, my older son and I decided to watch the original version of "Lilo and Stich" for our "Mommy, Clay Bae Date Night." I was starting to doze off as the older sister rocked Lilo to sleep when I heard Clay's quiet voice crack asking, "If you and dad die, will I have to take care of Jed all by myself?" The question caught me completely off guard, and I resisted the urge to scoff it off by saying something like, "Dad and I aren't going to die!!!" I have a very sensitive and intuitive little boy, and I recognized this question came from a deeper curiosity and concern.

I took a deep breath and said, "Honey, if dad and I passed away now, there are many people who love you and would care for you BOTH because you are both little boys. You would not be responsible for taking care of yourself, let alone your little brother. But one day dad and I will grow older and pass away and it MAY just be you and Jed. But mommy and daddy will figure out what that can look like and, when you become an adult, you can enter the conversation if you'd like to. But here's what I KNOW for sure—you and Jed love each other like Lilo and her sister! The bond you have is strong and beautiful. Mommy doesn't have any siblings and I am in awe of the relationship you and Jed have. It's special. We are ohana and ohana means family!!! That's never going to change."

He wiped a tear from his face and said, "I'm Jed's big brother and I will always look after him."

My heart swelled knowing the depth of the love between them. Growing up as an only child, this instant bond between my boys was a beautiful phenomenon to witness. I also began to worry at this moment that Clay might be worrying prematurely about what will happen to his brother if we are not around. It's a delicate dance on our part of encouraging our older son's desire to nurture while not impressing upon him that he has to do anything other than be a good brother to Jed.

One night, Jed was crying uncontrollably. The kind of cry that makes a mother double over in pain because she knows it's a plea for help. During this moment in time, I would have moved heaven and earth to take away what was wrong, but I kept coming up short. Tears of desperation were forming in my eyes when Clay walked in, of his own accord. He started singing the words to a lullaby we sing each night before bed. I started to join in, but he softly said, "Mom, I want to do this." I zipped my lips and listened and watched. Clay knelt down in front of his younger brother and wrapped his arms around him while singing slowly. Thoughtfully. Intentionally. Within seconds, Jed had stopped crying and was leaning into his brother.

It was the most magnificent thing I've ever seen. Nobody asked Clay to do this and, once Jed calmed down, Clay left the room as quickly as he'd come in. Yet, in those few minutes, the tone shifted and peace permeated all four walls. All was well. It made me wonder if it will always be this way between the two of them . . .

This past summer, Clay asked my husband about marriage, wondering aloud if every person HAS to get married. My husband told him that not everyone gets married and reminded him that he has a long time to decide whether or not he wants to have a spouse or family of his own. Without skipping a beat, Clay said, "I don't know if I want to get married but I know I want Jed to live with me." I've heard many parents further down this path say that their other children opted to care for their sibling with a disability without any prior nudging. This may not be the case for every family, nor does it need to be. But the love shared between siblings can be a sacred and beautiful one, as described next.

Brother Do You Love Me?

By Manni Coe, Author of "Brother. Do. You. Love. Me," Brother and Advocate in the Down syndrome community

Reuben is the youngest of four brothers and he was born with Up (Down) syndrome. We are not allowed to call it Down syndrome anymore, at least not in my family.

I am brother number two and as our two other brothers married and had children of their own, life kind of threw Reuben and I together. One thing was clear; my late father wanted to make sure that Reuben had gained his legs of independence way before my parents' old age. My father had read somewhere that people with Down syndrome process grief in a very acute way, sometimes taking years to process the death of a parent. So my father was adamant that Reuben lived independently from them from his early twenties. Not because he didn't love him but precisely because he did!

Back in 2019, when Reuben was 36, his life in a care home or supported living facility looked great on paper. A team of carers to look after him, care plans, activities, one-to-one time with his key worker. What could possibly go wrong? In all eventuality, everything went wrong. Reuben adopted a passive role due to over-caring. He was stripped of decision-making. Stripped of even risk assessed free time to roam a village or a shopping center. His creativity began to dissipate as we saw his life experience diminish. And then . . . the COVID-19 pandemic hit. Already in a precarious sense of well-being, Reuben began to sink into a non-verbal, psychological regression and depression. We couldn't get to him. He wasn't allowed any visitors. He began to disappear.

Then in November of 2020, he sent me a now famous text message which was a brave and deliberate cry for help.

"brother. do. you. love. me."

Those five words changed the tangent of our lives and instigated a sibling rescue mission, a subsequent book deal, and a whole series of life-changing events. I always say that seeing the return of Reuben's smile has been the greatest privilege of my life. He was broken. He was a wounded bird that I had to bring out of the cold and begin to gently breathe life back into him. What neither of us realized is that I was also breathing life back into me.

And this is where our brotherhood is symmetrical. Reuben needed me to save him but in his quiet wisdom, I believe he also knew he was saving me.

Reading Manni's book last summer filled my heart with hope for the future of my boys and reminded me of the sacred nature of their relationship. And yet, the dynamic of having both a typical and neurotypical child can be difficult to navigate for the parents. As they grow, the sibling of a child with a disability may begin to feel overlooked, ignored, or "seen through" by their caregivers. Especially if there are multiple hospital stays or regular instances of illness that require the highest form of care and attention by the parents.

This child is often referred to as a "glass child." Alicia Meneses Maples coined the term "glass child" in her 2010 TEDx Talk, which brought attention to children who feel invisible because their siblings require significant parental attention. Maples, who grew up with a brother who had autism and another with a terminal illness, said the term "glass" refers to the fact that these children are often overlooked, not that they are fragile. In these cases, the sibling may suppress their own emotions and needs, becoming an independent or self-sacrificing caretaker. It's important to note that this is not an official or formal diagnosis but a way of describing an emotional experience of a child who may find themselves in this kind of circumstance.

If a family is worried they may be facing a scenario like this, it's crucial to open the door to communication and frequent expression of the feelings of their child. For parents, it may feel like an impossible goal to balance their time with their children. Kate Eshleman,

PSyD, says in an article written by Jenn Lonzer, "It's an incredibly difficult situation. We can all identify with the fact that there are a finite number of hours in the day. And there's only so much you can get done in those hours. When parents are in impossible situations like this, they have to prioritize."[2]

How can parents do this?

- Ask for help BEFORE you burn out.
- Avoid asking too much of the sibling (particularly tasks that aren't age appropriate).
- Carve out time for each child (even a few minutes a day).
- Tell your child you wish you could spend more time with them, even when you can't.
- Find support for yourself and for your child (therapies, organizations, workshops, etc.).

There can be an unspoken or unidentified resentment, jealousy, or inward struggles that the sibling carries and, when this happens, the caregiver has the opportunity to seek a counselor or support group for them. There are resources available within the Down syndrome community for these types of scenarios. For instance, at the National Down Syndrome Congress (NDSC) Convention every summer, there is a sibling support group offered where lifelong friendships and connections are forged. It's a safe space to connect, share struggles and triumphs, and find others who understand more of your personal experience. These types of resources also exist in many local GiGi's Playhouses throughout the country. A sibling doesn't ever have to face hardships alone.

Parents can also struggle to balance their attention between children and that doesn't always mean an imbalance of attention as mentioned with Glass Child Syndrome. A common trap parents fall into is comparing the child with Down syndrome to their typical siblings (I've heard this story more than a dozen times with twins, in particular, where one has Down syndrome and the other does not). Milestones that often come easily to a typical child, may take a little (or a lot) longer for a child with Down syndrome. THAT IS OK. Children with Down syndrome have a different genetic makeup and that may contribute to some delays according to the typical charts. Just like any individual, your child with Down syndrome will have strengths and weaknesses that determine when/where/how a milestone is reached. Many in our community call them "inchstones" instead of milestones because growth can happen slowly and with the tiniest bits of progress. But progress is progress is progress is progress.

We shouldn't feel the need to compare our own children because they are not the same people. It is our job, as parents, to provide consistent and impactful support that is uniquely fashioned to them, in order to set our child up for success. Once we've done that, we can let THEM set the pace. So many times I have thought to myself, Jed might never get this or do this or say that . . . and he comes out of left field and knocks something out of the park. Patience and persistence are the keys to triumph. And bit by bit, our children grow, evolve, change, and spread their wings in their own lives.

When this kind of evolution begins to occur, children may go off to go to college or leave "the nest." Here is some great advice from a Board-certified medical geneticist and co-author of *Common Threads: Celebrating Life with Down Syndrome* and *Fasten Your Seatbelt: A Crash Course on Down Syndrome for Brothers and Sisters*:

> "When a sibling heads off to college, life at home can feel different for the whole family especially for people with Down syndrome. This big milestone brings both challenges and opportunities, and with love and connection, families can grow even stronger through the change. It's important to explain to the person with Down syndrome that their sibling is going away to college but not gone forever. It's good to have a memento or keepsake or a photo to keep in their bedroom that their brother or sister is still very much in their lives. Utilize video conferences or FaceTime to have chats with their siblings to remind them that they are still there and still a part of their lives. It's also important for parents to have an honest conversation with the sibling moving away. You don't want an extra burden placed on them of having to check in to talk to their brother and sister so they can have

the space they want and not always have the guilt of not always checking in. It's a fine tuned balance between sibling relationships."[3]

There is a lot to consider with sibling relationships and there is not a one-size-fits-all for any of this. Life is full of twists and turns that can be difficult to navigate. Each family has their own way of being and each day, you will figure it out together. Let the love between all of you guide the process and remember what Carolina has to say.

A Sisterly Bond

By Carolina, Sister and Advocate in the Down syndrome community

I was 12 years old and my brother, Ernesto, was 15 years old when our sister Angelica was born with Down syndrome in 1996. My mom's doctor said to terminate because Angelica wouldn't have a great life. But let me tell you, he was so wrong, and Angelica has the greatest life of anybody I know. This girl knows how to party and live life to the fullest, no matter where she is.

I was a fortunate sibling, able to be the baby of the family for 12 years, and then, when Angelica was born and a few years later when our brother went to college, I became the oldest in our home, which was an entirely new role I never thought I'd have, but it certainly has been the greatest. My brother picked on me, so wait . . . did that mean I could pick on my sister? It sure did!! That's my sibling—Down syndrome or not. I get to have the typical relationship everyone else has with their siblings. Sure, Angelica and I might not share clothes like typical sisters, and I couldn't tell her about my marriage troubles that finally led to my divorce because she wouldn't understand, but my goodness, whenever I needed to smile, I knew I just needed to call her, and I'd be better in that moment.

I lived at home while I went to college. I would drive to class, come home, and watch Barney and The Wiggles with

Angelica, and I loved it. Ahhh, 2004, what a time. I was studying journalism at Arizona State to be a reporter, and that road eventually led to the possibility of an internship at MTV in Los Angeles. Could I leave my sister? I really didn't know. I struggled with that for a bit. What is she going to do if I leave? Looking back, I'm proud of my 21-year-old self for seizing the opportunity because 20 years later, Angelica is just fine. In fact, if anyone has enjoyed my work perks, it's been her!

One of my favorite parts of being a sibling to a person with Down syndrome is social media. I know, right? I guess it just depends on how you use it. When I first moved to LA and interned at MTV in 2006, Facebook was beginning to let people other than college students join. Angelica had come to visit MTV, and everyone loved her. Then, people got to see how completely typical our sibling relationship is through my posts and pictures over the years. So much so that she eventually helped influence some of the coolest people in the entertainment industry to do great things for our community through representation. From TV programs to presenter slots on award shows, if what I think is a simple picture of me and Angelica out to dinner can help show someone that she's living a great life, then yeah. That's awesome. There is absolutely nothing down about Down syndrome.

I wouldn't be who I am today without Angelica. She shaped me. She drives me crazy, too. But she's shown me patience and kindness and quickness and laughter and love. Most of all, love. If you just got the diagnosis for Down syndrome and you're wondering about how that might affect your other children, they're going to be ok. Is it going to be easy? No. But neither would a typical younger sibling. I promise you, a baby with Down syndrome is only going to make everything so much better. They will teach you things you will never ever learn in a book. Angelica will always be my favorite person, and I couldn't be luckier to have her as my sister.

A Little Extra

I feel one of the most important things I can do as a mother to my two little boys is encourage and uplift them for their unique gifts. No two people are the same and, even when children live under the same roof, there are significant differences. We can let go of the pressure of having to make carbon copies out of them. Without a doubt, your children will grow and learn from one another, simply by living together and growing together. That is a truly beautiful thing and something to ENJOY!

CHAPTER 8

What on Earth Is an IEP?

> *"Every child has a different learning style and pace. Each child is unique, not only capable of learning but also capable of succeeding."*
>
> —Robert John Meehan

IEP . . . Another abbreviation! OY! Just when I thought I'd mastered them all and unlocked the riddles that once seemed unsolvable, another one came. So, what on Earth is an IEP and how can you stay informed as a parent?

An IEP is an Individualized Education Plan for students who are receiving special education in school. For children three years or older, contact your local elementary school or school district to request an evaluation. Your child can be evaluated even if they do not attend public school. IEPs are offered in every state but each state has its own rules for how IEPs are implemented. This is a legally binding agreement that the team makes, which includes you as the parent. Together, you are creating a document that lays out, specifically, how your child will have free and appropriate public education within the least restrictive environment.

In a nutshell:

An IEP is a document that outlines the learning needs of your child and how those needs will be tackled.

- It ensures that your child with a disability will have the opportunity to be in general education curriculum and what types of support needs to be in place for that to happen.
- An IEP includes goals, accommodations, and specialized services.

The process for creating an IEP begins when a teacher, parent, or doctor notices a student may be struggling. A referral is made to the school's counselor or psychologist.

The school psychologist often completes an evaluation and presents their findings. Eligibility must be decided by the full IEP team during the formal eligibility/initial determination meeting (the terminology varies by state). The decision is made using multiple data sources: evaluation results, teacher input, parent input, outside evaluations, classroom data, and observations. Pre-determination is not allowed under IDEA and the school should not decide in advance whether a student qualifies; the team must make that decision collaboratively by reviewing all data together during the meeting.

If the student qualifies, a team of professionals meets to create the IEP.

IEPs can vary by state:

- Each state has a variance in the laws and regulations that specify what information must be included in your child's IEP.
- Each state may also decide how to format the IEP.

IEPs can be considered a road map, of sorts, to help your child and all those who work with them. You, as the parent, are an equal and valued member of the child study team and they help guide the direction of the meetings and outcomes. Keep in mind that these plans can and WILL change. Nothing is set in stone and they are meant to grow, change, and adapt as your child grows, changes, and adapts. Here's a more in-depth look at the process of an IEP.

The IEP Process and Data Collection

The IEP process is comprised of the following steps:

1. Referral for a special education evaluation for your loved one
2. Evaluating your child's eligibility for special education services
3. Scheduling the IEP meeting
4. Developing the initial IEP for your child
5. Providing special education and related services for your child
6. Monitoring your loved one's progress
7. Reviewing your child's IEP and performing reevaluation as needed

IEP data collection is a way for teachers to keep track of your child's progress and assess the progress of the goals your team set in the IEP. The information collected during an IEP process may include but is not exclusive to, your child's attendance, behavior, academics, social/emotional, and other focus areas. These data points help your IEP team make informed decisions around your loved one's educational experience.

This system is beneficial to teachers, parents, and guardians in making sure the child is taking steps toward their goals and learning in the most suitable environment for them. If it's discovered that extra support may be necessary, teachers can work toward implementing those changes. This process provides an objective way to report your child's progress to YOU, the caregiver.

Defining student IEP goals allows the team to:

- Better understand student progress.
- Define the method for data collection and tracking.
- Aid special education teachers in providing an optimal learning experience.

An IEP should also provide information on addressing a child's disability and special education needs, enabling them to participate and make progress in the general education curriculum. It's truly the foundational element that makes sure the entire team is on the same page. The IEP team should keep track of a student's progress and make informed decisions more effectively if goals are hinged on the child's present level of academic achievement and functional performance.

Tips for Improving Your IEP Data Collection

A solid IEP data collection system is aligned to SMART goals and involves the following:

- Writing measurable IEP goals and objectives
- Collecting data together by relevance
- Collecting data that is related to an attainable goal
- Having a relevant data collection system and timely data collection
- Analyzing trends present in the collected data

This process is made easier by breaking things down into categories (see Figure 8.1). Before walking into any IEP meeting, you can feel empowered and prepared by keeping these measurable goals in mind.

Here's what I might say to myself: "Misty, what's the best way for you to communicate your hopes for Jed with the rest of his team? What can you do ahead of time to ensure that your concerns are voiced in a clear and meaningful way?"

Are your thoughts and goals:

- **Specific.** Goals should be clear and straightforward, identifying what needs to be accomplished, who is accountable, and the definite steps to achieve it.
- **Measurable.** Goals should be quantitative and reflect trackable benchmarks.
- **Attainable.** Goals should be created based on the specifics of the student's situation and be attainable, while still being challenging.
- **Relevant.** Goals should align with the student's needs and identify the reason why such goals and objectives are necessary.

- **Time-based.** Goals should indicate the key milestones like data collection dates and the target date that they should be achieved.

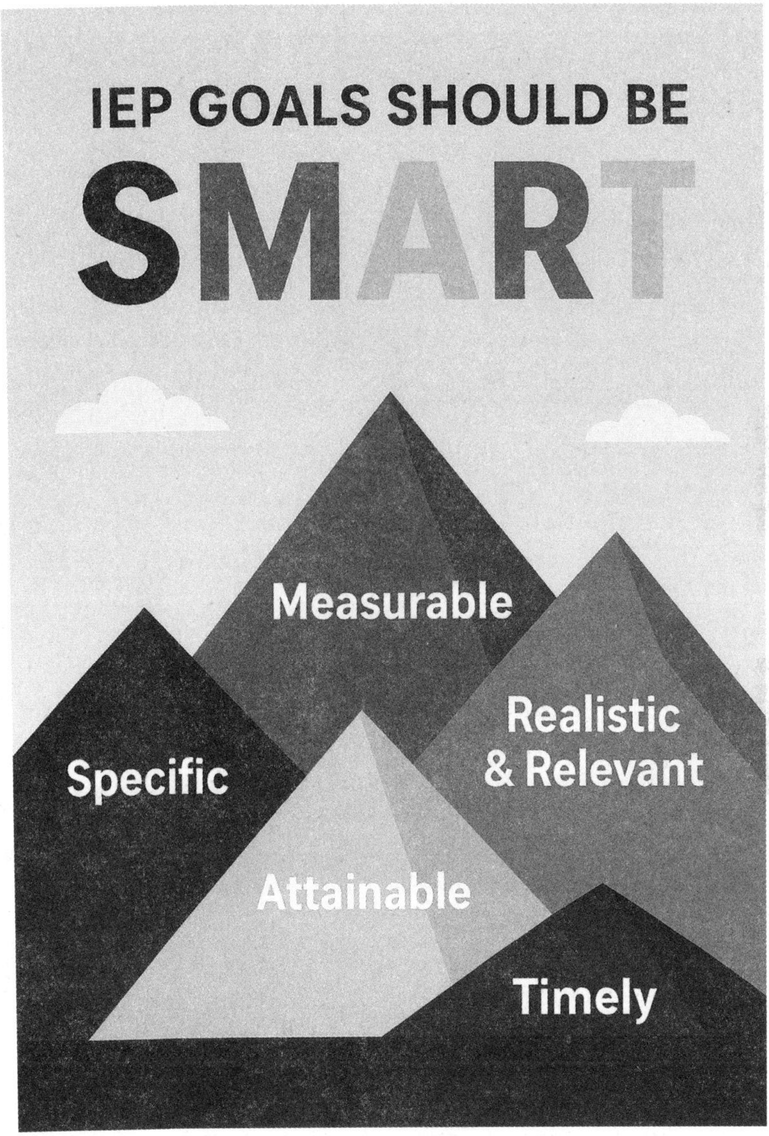

Figure 8.1 A visual of SMART goals by Tiffany Abbott Fuller

Once your child is over 14 (in some states, it's 12 and up), they need to have a transition section of the IEP that is specifically for transition planning. There should be goals set out specifically surrounding that transition, such as these:

- What does the child want to do?
- What do they want to study?
- What school do they want to go to?
- How are they going to work toward independence?

The most effective IEPs are built around your child's strengths. That can seem counterintuitive because teams are taught to create IEPs that signal a child needing special education. Due to that, there can be an overemphasis on deficits and weaknesses. But if a child's eligibility for an IEP has already been determined, there should be a focus on strengths. The team should presume competence, assume capabilities, and identify supports to help the child reach their goals and work toward their full potential.

As the parent, it's important to remember that you hold a lot of power at this table. Your voice shapes the plan. YOU are an expert when it comes to your child and only you know what he does or doesn't do at home. Only you know what he does or doesn't do during extracurricular activities or family outings. Your unique role is vital in building a bridge WITH their expertise in their respective fields. Working together can only be successful when both sides of the table understand and respect what the other side has to offer.

Carly Durham is a Nurse Practitioner, special education/disability advocate, and parent of children with Down syndrome. She writes and speaks about navigating the special education system, promoting inclusive practices, and supporting families of children with intellectual and developmental disabilities. She's a Certified Master IEP Coach®, a graduate of TCDD Partners in Policymaking, and a member of COPAA. She works to make the system more accessible and empowering for all children.

Empowering Parents

By Carly Durham, NP, Special Education/Disability Advocate, and Parent

An IEP works best when families feel confident using their voice. No one brings more insight, history, or hope to the table than a parent advocating for their child. The most effective IEPs don't start with deficits; they start with strengths. When teams presume competence and build support around what a child can do, real growth becomes possible.

If the IEP doesn't sound like your child, it's absolutely appropriate AND IMPORTANT to say so. Your perspective matters, and you have every right to make sure your view is reflected in the record. Collaboration almost always leads to better outcomes than conflict. While there are rare situations where intentions may be concerning, most challenges in IEP meetings come from misunderstandings or gaps in knowledge about policy or procedure, not from ill will. When we avoid assuming bad intentions from team members, we create an environment where everyone can stay focused on the child instead of slipping into an unhelpful "us versus them" dynamic.

One of the most powerful tools a parent has is the ability to ask thoughtful, effective questions. You don't have to do all the talking. Staying curious invites the team to show their reasoning, provide the data, explain alternatives, and demonstrate how they reached their decisions. When we respond with questions rather than immediate reactivity, conversations stay centered on impact, clarity, and solutions.

And above all, your child's worth is never contingent on benchmarks, scores, or goals. They are worthy exactly as they are. The IEP is simply one piece of the puzzle that supports their access to education; it does not define, limit, or measure their inherent value.

There are many other voices and observations added to an IEP so you, as an equal and important member of the team, also deserve to have your voice officially captured in the document. As you prepare for your next annual IEP, be empowered by the advice of Carly and prepare a ***Parent Input Statement.*** This is just another way of describing a letter written by *you,* the parent, about your insights, concerns, and desired areas of focus pertaining to your child. It's great to begin by acknowledging and thanking the team for their work with your child. You can highlight particular areas of growth you've noticed and express your appreciation for continued cultivation of relationships with teachers and therapists.

In the following section(s), you can express your vision for your child and name the areas you hope to change or adapt. You can list your goals and propose ways for the team to rally around your child to help the goals become achievable. This could be anything from cultivating relationships with typical peers, encouraging independence in and around the classroom, to academic goals and milestones. This letter is the place to express your unique perspective and expertise when it comes to the child you are raising.

A Little Extra

Going into an IEP meeting and preparing a Parent Input Letter can be intimidating, especially for the first time. The more you are able to walk in prepared and ready, the more you will be set up for success. Whether or not the school asks you for your input and regardless of any pushback you may experience, please know that it's a legal part of the IEP. The IDEA states that the parent's concerns are officially a part of any Individualized Education Plan.

(OH NO, another abbreviation! IDEA stands for the Individuals with Disabilities Education Act, a US federal law that provides rights and protections to students with disabilities and ensures they receive a free and appropriate public education. It mandates that eligible children receive special education and related services tailored to their individual needs.)

As the child's caregiver, you can call for an IEP meeting any time you feel like something needs to be adjusted or further looked into (bearing in mind that the team can't always instantly snap their fingers and make this meeting happen). And, again, If you feel that something is off or not working, you are an equal and important member of the team.

CHAPTER 9

To Include or Not Include? That Is the Question

"The world needs different kinds of minds to work together."
—Temple Grandin

Throughout my formative years in school, I was trying to fit in and "fit the mold," whatever that meant! If it hadn't been for the performing arts, I might never have found my voice. I could have easily become a vapid, perfectionistic, check all the boxes kind of person. Theater kept me grounded and created an environment that fostered my creativity. It also helped me open my mind to different types of people and a variety of experiences that varied from my own. And yet, I didn't have a single person with Down syndrome in any of my classes throughout my schooling.

Did you? If so, I'd venture to say you are in the minority.

Yet, somehow, since the moment Jedidiah was born, I've heard everyone around me shouting about the importance of inclusion. It dawned on me, early on, that I am expected to fight for something for my child with Down syndrome that I never saw modeled when I was growing up. If there were individuals with disabilities at my school, they weren't in my classes. That realization was overwhelming because I didn't know HOW to fight for inclusion.

More importantly, I didn't know WHY. Or what it even looked like, practically. My questions included the following:

- **WHY fight for inclusion?** The Individuals with Disabilities Education Act (IDEA) recommends that students with disabilities be taught in the Least Restrictive Environment (LRE).
- **But what does that actually mean?** Students with disabilities should be taught in the general education setting for the maximum amount of time possible with the necessary support to help them learn. The goal driven by federal policy is 80% of the day in a general education setting.
- **But what about the typical students? How will they be impacted?** Numerous studies and a vast array of lived experiences have shown that non-disabled students can benefit from sharing the classroom with those who have learning differences. These students either show improved academic and social outcomes, or their outcomes remain the same. **(Science Direct Educational Research Review, Volume 21: June 2017**—Academic achievement of students without special educational needs in inclusive classrooms: A meta-analysis).

So what are the potential gains of a least restrictive environment? They include the following:

- **Speech and language:** Children with Down syndrome who are taught in their mainstream school setting with support display significant language growth over time, in both structure and clarity. Speech and language skills influence all aspects of social and emotional development and impact a person's ability to make friends and participate with community and family.
- **Access to the curriculum alongside peers:** Full inclusion in the curriculum leads to higher literacy and number skills, and general knowledge.
- **Optimal learning environment:** Children with disabilities need to learn shoulder to shoulder with their typical peers

with the necessary supports in place. Data shows that children learn most effectively from their typically developing peers.

- **Friendships:** With the help of parents and teachers, friendships between neurotypical and neurodiverse children can carry on outside of the school setting. These relationships, if fostered, can grow and develop into their later years, and a broader understanding and appreciation of adults with Down syndrome is a natural by-product. That has long-lasting impact.
- **Long-term confidence in society:** Children with Down syndrome will experience the most growth when they are accepted and celebrated in school and society. This will improve confidence, self-esteem, and a general feeling of support. Parents and teachers need to do more to ensure that friendships with non-disabled peers carry on outside of school. An improvement in understanding and support for teenagers and adults with Down syndrome in their homes, workplaces, shops, and leisure activities could be one of many positive results from inclusion.

When the whole school gets involved in setting the tone for diversity, the outcome becomes acceptance, love, and appreciation for those who may act or look differently than you do. It takes a village to facilitate change and create environments that foster inclusion.

Let's dive further into the idea of inclusive education since this is a topic that is new to many of us!

Some History

By Sue Buckley, Gillian Bird, Ben Sacks and Tamsin Archer, as published in Down Syndrome News and Update

"The right to inclusive education is currently supported by the Least Restrictive Environment (LRE) section in Part B of the Individuals with Disabilities Education Act (IDEA). The right to

(*continued*)

equal access to a free and appropriate public education (FAPE) was introduced in the U.S. with the enactment of Public Law 94-142 in 1975, the precursor to IDEA. Research across decades has demonstrated that the proportion of students with Down syndrome who attend inclusive schools has varied greatly across different districts, and the overall trend was for students with Down syndrome in inclusive settings to transfer into segregated classes at some point during their school career. Research over the past 20 years indicates that successful inclusion from early years through higher and continuing education is not conditional on the ability or behavior of the child. Instead, it is dependent on the school's ability to accommodate and support the individual within the community and the structures of the educational setting. In turn, this depends on the school team having positive attitudes toward individuals with Down syndrome and believing inclusion is a right. With practice, outcomes in inclusive settings can improve for this group of students. Socially, schools can provide daily opportunities for students with Down syndrome to mix with typically developing peers, learn from models for age-appropriate behavior and develop relationships with young people from their community. Successful inclusion is a key step toward enabling children with Down syndrome to become full and contributing members of the community, and society reaps the benefits. Students and the wider school community gain skills and knowledge about how to understand, support and include people with disabilities. Typically developing peers gain an understanding of diversity, disability and tolerance through being part of an inclusive school community."

One particular study done in 2000 compared the achievements of teenagers of similar ability and family background educated in special schools and mainstream settings. The study showed significant educational benefits for teenagers who had been through mainstream education with 25–30 hours of additional learning support assistance. The teenagers who had been fully included in mainstream classes showed gains of more than two years in spoken language skills and three years in reading and writing ability on standardized measures. This study is described in full in "A comparison of mainstream and special education for teenagers with Down syndrome: implications for parents and teachers."[1]

In black and white, studies back up the importance of inclusion from an early age when it comes to individuals with Down syndrome. But sometimes lived experience doesn't pan out the way studies show. Each person is an individual with nuanced experiences, each unique and valuable. Therefore, each parent and child has to do what is best for them. Take Angela and her daughter Casey, for instance.

Learning on the Job

By Angela O'Brien, Parent Advocate, Podcast Host

If you're anything like me, you've wished your children came with a personalized manual—one that tells you when your daughter needs a hug or a snack, or how your son felt at recess today, and whether he's dreading tomorrow's doctor visit. For our children with Down Syndrome, challenges with verbal and language skills make that terrain even harder to navigate. If only someone could invent a thought translator for our kids—imagine how many heartaches and tears that would save.

Casey Jane, our lively but somewhat introverted 22-year-old with Down Syndrome, has always struggled to express herself verbally. When she does speak, I have to look at her closely, concentrating to understand whether she's quoting a favorite Austin & Ally episode or sharing something truly important. Even though her speech is difficult to understand, she knows when I understand her—and I know almost immediately when

(*continued*)

I don't. Somehow, that frustration comes through loud and clear.

So, I was taking a bit of a chance when, one sunny Friday afternoon, I asked her about her new school and whether she missed her old friends as we cruised up the Tollway. She was just finishing her second week at a brand-new school, mid-way through fifth grade. I could tell she was thinking hard about my question.

"I don't have those words," she whispered—so quietly I worried I'd embarrassed or shamed her.

She had never said anything so profound. The move to a new school mid-year, just a few months after puberty, couldn't have come at a more confusing time. Of course she didn't have the words to describe how she felt. I drove the rest of the way home in silence, stealing glances at her at every traffic light, looking for any little sign—a slight smile, a relaxed shoulder—something to calm my anxious heart and reassure me that uprooting her entire community overnight had been worth it.

Up until that point, we were, in most people's eyes, living the special needs parent dream: a comfortable suburban home on a tree-lined street, young families everywhere, parks and pools within walking distance. Our respected public elementary school had not only welcomed my older, typically developing son, but also embraced my daughter—their first student with Down Syndrome—from day one of kindergarten. (Not without a lot of work on our part, but that's a story for another day.) I even befriended three other neighborhood moms whose daughters also had Down Syndrome. I had to pinch myself.

We spent those elementary years building trust and mutual respect with the school staff. They understood how important inclusion was to us and shared our dream that Casey would one day graduate from the local high school alongside her peers. These teachers were genuinely invested in her success.

But puberty cracked open an anxiety none of us saw coming. From the first day of fifth grade, she began to notice her differences. She asked why her assignments looked different from the others.' She grew frustrated when she was the only one pulled out of math class. Her happy-go-lucky demeanor faded. She grew quieter after school. Homework often ended in tears—sometimes hers, sometimes mine—followed by a message to her teacher explaining why the assignment wasn't done. Our girl was withering in front of our eyes, and none of us knew how to help. My husband and I put our heads together and started thinking outside the box. There was a school downtown known for serving kids with intellectual disabilities, but that would mean no more "inclusion." Was that even an option?

Since the week she was born, I'd been taught that inclusion was the only option. When my obstetrician invited another family—parents of an older child with Down Syndrome—to meet me in the hospital, I was barely 24 hours postpartum, holding my brand-new baby as they told me how to "fight for inclusion." (For the record: 0/10, do not recommend that timing.) The rest of the conversation is a blur, but that message stuck. Every conference, seminar, and parent group I attended afterward said the same thing: inclusion was the gold standard, and anything less was a failure. The idea of choosing a specialized school filled me with guilt.

But something inside us told us to really listen, not to other parents, teachers, or experts, but to our daughter. What harm could come from just making a phone call?

We agreed to let her shadow for a day. She'd been working on a little "About Me" project for her fifth-grade class—a project she refused to present in her general education setting. I quietly tucked that paper into her backpack, hoping the teachers might see it and use it as a window into who she was while she explored this bright and cheery school of students, many of whom looked a lot like her.

By the end of that day, she had read her project aloud to the entire class and climbed into my car with a smile I hadn't seen in weeks. I knew then and there: we had found her school home.

(*continued*)

As I write this, my daughter is about to graduate from that school, after 10 years in a community that values her. Ten years of building practical job skills, forming true friendships that didn't end at 3 p.m. on Fridays, and learning to speak up for herself. She couldn't do that back in fifth grade when she needed a change. She literally didn't have the words.

Luckily, her father and I have learned to read her in other ways, our own "Casey translator," if you will. She never gives up a smile unless it's genuine. Her waving hands and rocking body scream excitement without any decibels. And if she's mad about not getting chicken nuggets for dinner again? You definitely know it.

Maybe we don't need anyone to invent a thought translator after all. Maybe it's something already inside us, waiting to be tuned in. Because while Casey has certainly benefited from expert advice over the years, there came a time when we had to tune out those outside voices and listen only to hers. What worked for other children with Down syndrome no longer worked for her. We just needed the courage to admit that and make the change that she needed.

So don't worry if you haven't developed your own "thought translator" yet. Ours took more than a decade to fully form. Just make sure that when it does, you use it for what it's meant for: helping your child's voice be heard—even when the world is drowning it out.

Angela and Casey's story is so important to emphasize because it demonstrates the importance of being attuned to the current needs and changes of your loved one. Nothing is stagnant, least of all people. Something might be right for a time and then change. Adaptability, flexibility, awareness, and communication are the keys to success on this path.

A Little Extra

This chapter was burning on my heart long before I began writing this book. As I mentioned earlier in the chapter, there can be a lot of pressure (whether internally or externally) to push for inclusion at all costs. Studies would suggest that inclusion is beneficial to our children, without a doubt. However, as in all aspects of this journey, it's crucial to keep an open mind to whatever the individual at hand may need. And, again, that may change from year to year or even month to month.

CHAPTER 10

Finding Your Voice for Advocating

> *"There is no greater disability in society than the inability to see a person as more."*
>
> —Robert M. Hensel

I was interviewed for a podcast about a year into my journey as a mom in the Down syndrome community. The host of the show began our episode by saying,

> "Some people would view this path you are walking with Jed as their worst case scenario."

At the time, the statement really took me aback and stung because he was talking about my son. . .my life. However, the more I reflected upon his statement, the more I realized that he was right. While so much progress has been made in areas of science, advocacy, inclusion, early intervention and education plans, the fact remains that there is a lot of fear and ableism surrounding Down syndrome.

Only once we've done the work of dismantling ableism and peeling back the layers of our own ingrained fear can we then begin to learn on the job and do the work of advocating! It's not a smooth ride, and there are certainly bumps and lessons to be gleaned along the way. But the silver lining of making mistakes is learning how NOT to do things. Sometimes real-world, real-time experience is more valuable than any advice given by a friend or words read off the pages of a book. That's why it's important to DIVE IN! The water may be rocky and deep at first, but eventually your body remembers that it can and WILL swim.

While the experiences of families in the disability community vary across the globe, many of the emotions and struggles are universal. Tonye, president and Founder of Simone's Oasis in Nigeria, shares the story of her daughter and the evolution of her own advocacy here.

Advocacy on a Global Scale

By Tonye, Author, Advocate and Mother in the Down syndrome community

How did I get here? I wasn't supposed to be here.

This wasn't meant to be my life. But somehow, I wouldn't change a thing. . .well, maybe I'd ask for a little more money (lol) but truly, I wouldn't change a thing.

Sometimes I think of the movie Sliding Doors, how one small moment, one choice, can split your world in two. What if you'd gone the other way? What if you'd caught that train, or missed it? I don't even know what I thought my life would look like, but I imagine it would've involved being some kind of high-flying TV executive, maybe a VP of something.

Not this.

Not this mum, this carer, this advocate. All-consuming, all-consumed.

Every day I think, What can I do to make this world just a little less cruel?

Just a little bit better for my daughter and others like her. But then I stop and wonder, how much can one person really do?

Perhaps I can try.

I can talk. I can speak. I can raise my voice.

I can tell our story. I can tell her story.

Simone.

How did I get here? I wasn't supposed to be here.

And yet, maybe I was. Maybe I am. Maybe it was always part of God's plan.

This year so much has happened that I can't believe, some call it synchronicity. Awards, international speaking engagements, two new books, newspaper articles, grant recipient, TV appearances, Simone's picture on world-famous billboards in New York and London. Somehow becoming a voice for the neurodiverse community, proudly Nigerian, proudly African, proudly carrying the flag, the t-shirt, the badge. . . special mum here, Down syndrome mum here, neurodiverse mum here.

But really, how did I get here? I wasn't supposed to be here. Not me. All this responsibility. The pressure. Could this be too much? I wonder and ponder. The same question I ask myself now, I asked myself nine years ago. . . but how things have changed.

I take a deep breath and let go of some of the anxiety and pressure I'm feeling. I ask myself really, was it wise to start my own foundation? Was it wise to take on this mission to raise awareness and advocate for children who otherwise would be discarded? Every day I'm drafting proposals, creating, consulting, advising, striving, trying. It's a struggle. Is all this really helping? I have to remind myself who I'm doing this for and why. Sometimes I just want to hide. Is anything I'm doing really helping others thrive? Today I'm typing this at my desk at home in Lagos. My son, doing homework in his room, comes out to ask me for a pen with a cheeky smirk (he has plenty in his room but wants one from my desk). I tease him and give him one. We laugh. My daughter screams and giggles as my husband chases her up the stairs. Joyful noise. I'm grateful. God, thank you, a reminder of my why in the midst of doubt.

Nine years ago, I was sitting beside a hospital bed, looking at my tiny, underweight, six-month-old baby girl with Down syndrome. I was pumping breast milk with one of those hospital-grade machines that looked like it was from the 1950s. I'd been

(*continued*)

pumping for weeks, freezing bottle after bottle. Simone was having open-heart surgery the next day.

I was terrified, so afraid, and so alone. I cried silently, quietly in the dark. I wept and asked God

Why?

This wasn't the plan. I wasn't supposed to be here. She wasn't supposed to be here. Not like this. This wasn't meant to be our story, Lord. The next three years felt like intense warfare. They say special needs parents carry trauma equivalent to combat veterans. I believe that.

Simone's healing process was long and arduous. We were far from home, two years in the U.S., one in the U.K. while my husband and son remained in Nigeria (apart from the occasional visit). My sole mission was her healing. I absorbed everything I could from her therapists and doctors. I fought for every bit of care, every referral, every ounce of respect. I was ghosted by social workers, dismissed by doctors, talked down to by those who should have known better. I encountered racism, both loud and quiet. Nothing came easy. But through it all, Simone and I became fiercely bonded.

What no one tells you when you get the diagnosis of Down syndrome is how it impacts your life in the most unexpected way. You're told about the burdens, the "cannots," the "will nots." You're not told about the joy, the laughter, the immense light and love this individual brings. I have never experienced a love like this, pure, divine, transformative. It breaks down walls and heals the soul. I remember one night in London, when everything felt like too much. Simone was two and asleep beside me. I was exhausted, bone-deep tired, crying silently in the dark. "Why, Lord? How am I supposed to do this? I can't. I need hope. I need help."

And then, suddenly, Simone sat up, and wrapped her tiny arms around me. She hugged me. I froze. I wept. I realized she was still sleeping, yet she'd somehow answered my prayer. It was my sign. God had heard me. I laid her back down, and she held onto my hand. I whispered, Thank you, over and over until

I fell asleep. A few months later, her cardiologist told us her heart function was normal. We could go home. To God be the glory.

Back in Nigeria, reunited as a family, it was wonderful. . .at first. My husband and the kids were happy, life settling back into rhythm. But inside, I felt. . . lost. Depression crept in. Who was I now? What was I supposed to do? The world had moved on without me. I couldn't get a job. I needed to be home with the kids, especially Simone. And even if I could work, who would hire me after so many years away? I'd spent years focused entirely on keeping my daughter alive. Now she was thriving. . . and I didn't know what to do with myself. I felt useless. I kept going through the motions; school runs, meals, bedtime, but I was numb and restless at the same time. It's a strange kind of emptiness.

How did I get here? I wasn't supposed to be here.

Still, I got up each day for my family. My husband kept telling me to be patient, to give myself space. I tried. I let go of expectations and slowly, by watching my children, their laughter, their light. . . healing began.

And then one day, purpose showed up in the form of a conversation with my son, Ugo.

Another Sliding Doors moment. He came home from school upset. "Mummy, it's not fair!" he said, indignant. come to play with Simone, but I'm not allowed to join!" I realized it was time to explain. I told him those people were Simone's therapists, and the "play" was actually therapy. I told him Simone had Down syndrome. "What's Down syndrome?" he asked.

That moment changed everything. I tried to explain chromosomes and oh, that was a disaster! "Mummy, what's a chro-chro-chro. . .?" He looked so confused. I reassured him Simone was fine, that she learned things in her own time, and that he could sit in the next session. He brightened up, but I knew I hadn't really answered him. I wanted a better way to explain. Books had always been a big part of our home, so I went online

(*continued*)

to find one. I searched and searched. The longer I searched, the more painful it became. It was like we were invisible. My family, our story, didn't exist in the world's imagination. Then the realization hit me: my daughter was the first Black person with Down syndrome I'd ever seen. I couldn't fix the world that day, but I could do something for my son. So I wrote a story, Ugo & Sim Sim: What is Down Syndrome? based on our own conversation, written the way I wished it had gone. I used my film and TV background to bring it to life, worked with an animation studio for illustrations, and printed two copies for my kids. When the kids saw themselves in those pages, they beamed, the first time I truly understood the power of representation.

"Mummy, this is me!" That was the first time I truly understood the power of representation. Not long after, a friend who also has a child with Down syndrome, came over. We caught up, cried, and compared stories. Ugo proudly showed her the book. She was stunned.

"Tonye, you can't keep this to yourself," she said. "Other families need this."

And she was right. That's how the Ugo & Sim Sim picture book series was born, the first in the world to feature a Black main character with Down syndrome. The journey wasn't easy. Nigerian publishers rejected me, saying that a book about a child with Down syndrome wouldn't sell. One even said no parent would buy "a book about an abomination." That word stung. But by then, I was battle-hardened. I knew better. I knew they were wrong. So I self-published. I learned everything from scratch, editing, printing, distribution. I poured my heart, time, and savings into it. When I finally printed those beautiful books, 100% made in Nigeria, I faced another wall: retailers who refused to stock them because they believed "Nigerian-made" meant "inferior." But families who read them told me otherwise. They saw their children in those pages. They saw hope.

That's when the idea for Simone's Oasis began to form. A virtual place of respite in the desert. A place of comfort, nourishment, and knowledge. I began creating videos, animations, and little pieces of content around Ugo and Sim Sim, and our real life. During the COVID pandemic, especially, these stories became a lifeline, for us and for others. None of it was planned. It all grew organically from what we were living. And through it, I began to dream again. If the world didn't have space for Simone, I would build one. Advocacy through storytelling became my calling, whether through books, animation, podcasts, music, or activities. All to make the world a little less cruel for Simone and others like her.

Now, Simone's Oasis stands as an organization advocating for children and people with Down syndrome, autism, and other neurodevelopmental challenges through creativity. We are changing mindsets in Nigeria and beyond, showing that disability isn't a curse, or sin, or something to be prayed away. There's still a long road ahead, but we've seen change. We've touched thousands of lives. We're proving that children with disabilities are not burdens, they're blessings. They can learn, work, contribute, and lead.

I know I'm blessed because I've found my purpose. Not just something I enjoy, but something I'm called to do. Purpose doesn't erase hardship; it gives you the strength to keep walking through it. It's not easy. But I draw strength from God, and from my home, my family, my light. Simone, this radiant being who continues to teach me about love, grace, and faith. Through her, I've connected with people all over the world, parents, advocates, dreamers, who walk in these same shoes. A beautiful, resilient community of understanding and courage. I don't know if there's a "point" to all these musings. Maybe there doesn't need to be. What I know is this: I am not the same woman I once was. I'm softer. Kinder. Stronger. Still transforming.

How did I get here? I wasn't supposed to be here.

Raising a child with Down syndrome has stretched and remade me in ways I never imagined. It's not comfortable, but it's deeply fulfilling. It opens your heart, again and again. Pulling you back, reminding you that love is the language to live by.

(*continued*)

So here I am. And for myself in looking back, I can finally look forward.

How did I get here? I wasn't supposed to be here.

And yet I know, to the very core of my being, I know: I am exactly where I'm meant to be.

Tonye and I spoke together at the UN in March of 2024, our first time meeting in person. On that day, we shared how amazing this journey of advocacy has been and we delighted in this mutual passion. A few years ago I began advocating and raising awareness for the Down syndrome community online. I didn't set out to do it, but I found myself compelled to share the joys of raising my precious Jed.

I also told a lot of HARD stories. Tales of ambulance rides and emergency rooms. I opened up in raw and vulnerable ways about medical debt we had accrued. I learned about the New Jersey Catastrophic fund that would pay 90% of our medical bills if we owed more than 10% of our annual income (which we did). I cried online when the mountains of paperwork seemed daunting and a medical grant we'd received proved to be unreliable. I also shared the horrors of encountering my first "trolls" when a reel of ours went viral.

Some of the comments made on the video, in addition to private messages I received, opened my eyes to the lack of education when it comes to disability. Sure, some people are just mean. But many times, people don't know what they don't know. I wanted to show them a real, true, living, breathing example of someone with Down syndrome in Jed. I desired to burst open the door of our home to expose the light and truth that indwelled there. This is how my advocacy began. Tonye expressed many of the same desires to me that day in March at the UN.

Over time, advocating begins to be a daily necessity. From navigating IEPs at my son's school to encountering difficult situations on the playground, my understanding and knowledge began to grow by leaps and bounds as I listened and learned from self-advocates with Down syndrome. I heard their message loud and clear when they talked about the desire to dismantle the negative connotations attached to the word "Disability." They taught me that there is nothing bad about the word. In fact, 20% of all people are disabled, and it's the largest minority group in the world. AND it's the only minority group in the world that anyone, anywhere can become a part of at any time. The word disability is nothing to fear. . .it's the negative connotations surrounding it that need to be reexamined and dissected.

Listening to self-advocates required reflection and contemplation. That work required a stiff, hard look at my own ableism.

As described by Keisha Greaves in an article entitled, "Understanding Ableism: How language Shapes Inclusion" by Northeast Arc,

> "Ableism refers to discrimination, prejudice, or systemic barriers that disadvantage disabled people. It can be overt, like denying someone a job because of their disability, or subtle, such as using language that reinforces harmful stereotypes. Addressing ableism is not just about big policy changes or accessibility laws; it's also about the way we communicate and the words we use. Many people don't realize that certain everyday phrases are rooted in ableism, and shifting our language can be an essential step toward creating a more inclusive society."[1]

Before we can begin to discuss what it might look like to advocate as a loved one of someone with Down syndrome, we have to first come together in acknowledging the ableism that is woven into the very fabric of our society. Every building without a ramp, every inaccessible playground, every reel on TikTok without closed captioning is a reminder that this world is not currently set up for those who live with disability. And those things are just physical reminders of what is lacking.

Here are forms of ableism broken down:

- **Social and attitudinal:**
  - Viewing disability as a defect rather than a part of human diversity.

  - Assuming people with disabilities are less worthy, less capable, or to be pitied.
  - Being patronizing or speaking to adults with disabilities as if they are children and referring to their needs as "special" instead of basic human needs.
  - Calling a person with a disability "inspirational" for completing everyday tasks.
- **Structural and systemic:**
  - Lack of accessible infrastructure, such as buildings without ramps or elevators.
  - Employers refusing to make reasonable accommodations.
  - Media portrayals that stereotype, mock or trivialize disabled characters.
- **Language:**
  - Using ableist terms in a derogatory way, such as "lame," "crazy," or "crippled." Saying a person's disability is "invisible," instead of acknowledging it is a part of who they are. An example of this might be, "Your son doesn't even look like he has Down syndrome! He is so cute. So normal looking."
- **Internalized ableism:**
  - Sense.org describes internalized ableism as the impact that living in an ableist society can have on disabled people. After being on the receiving end of ableism or disablism, you might feel low self-esteem or a sense of shame about your disability. Some call this internalized ableism. It's important to remember that you deserve respect and dignity, and you have rights like everyone else.[2]

Once we've acknowledged that there is a lot of work to do in making a more accessible and accepting society for ALL to coexist, we can then begin to peel back the ableism within our own hearts. Before we become defensive and shout, "I'm not ableist, I LOVE disabled people," think about one of the most common statements a pregnant mother hears—something along the lines of, "It doesn't matter if it's a girl or a boy, as long as the baby is healthy." It seems like an innocent statement, right? Who doesn't want their baby to be healthy?

The problematic nature of this statement becomes exposed when a baby is born who isn't "healthy" or typical. Maybe they have a chronic condition or they were born with a disability. Maybe that baby has Down syndrome. "As long as the baby is healthy" takes on a different tone when this happens. Especially for the parents who hear that statement echoing in their minds. Is their baby somehow less valuable? Less precious? Less worthy of dignity, respect, and care? Of course not! And yet, we as a society, act, speak and function as though disability is a tragedy.

But the tragedy doesn't lie with the disabled individual. The tragedy lies with the preconceived notions and constructs we've lived with and accepted for a long time without even being aware of what we are thinking or doing. And if we, as parents of children with Down syndrome, continue to carry those notions in our minds and hearts, we will forever be trying to fit our child into a box of "typical." We will always be trying to force a square peg into a round hole instead of letting our child possess four sides. The way they were designed.

Don't get me wrong. There are reasons to worry and grieve when your child suffers or struggles. We wouldn't be parents if we didn't want to protect our children from pain and suffering. But it's important to remember:

1. No parent can protect their children from suffering. It's a part of the human experience and no person is exempt from it.
2. We can't jump to the conclusion that people with Down syndrome or any disability are in a state of suffering. Especially when the statistics (covered in an earlier chapter) say otherwise. More often than not, it's our own mental biases and blockades that prevent us from seeing the beauty of neurodiversity.

I realized I'd grown up in a world that absolutely (whether spoken or unspoken) pitied those who were disabled. I was a loyal member of that club, once upon a time. I shudder when I think of a few times I dodged walking past a person with Down syndrome because I didn't know how to interact or what to say. I was blissfully unaware of my ignorance. In my High School days, the "R" word was a part of my vocabulary in describing activities I didn't like or a state of being of someone I wasn't too fond of. Reflecting back on how I used to be, not all that long ago, can be painful. But it's necessary work to unravel the years of damage I was doing to myself and others. I want to have eyes, wide open, for the future of Jedidiah and others like him.

As the mother of a child with Down syndrome, my personal advocacy often looks like pointing to truth through reels and posts on social media. Sometimes it comes in the form of speaking at a conference or at the United Nations. Many times, it looks like speaking face-to-face or over the phone with expecting parents who have just received a diagnosis. But the advocacy journey is personal and specific to you! No two advocates look the same, because no two people are the same! My background is in performance, speaking, and writing. I USE those gifts and abilities and training to advocate for my son. YOU might be a nurse who knows how to speak up in certain tense medical situations that would leave someone like me, speechless. Or maybe you are a lawyer who knows how to fight a case of discrimination that has left the parents feeling powerless. No matter who you are or where you come from, YOU have been given specific abilities that come in handy for advocating or raising awareness.

Here are some more examples:

- Writing a letter to congress
- Protesting locally or on a national level
- Speaking up on the news
- Reading a book about Down syndrome to your child's kindergarten class
- Joining the PTO to make sure a representative of the disability community has a voice there
- Hosting an event for parents experiencing burnout in the disability community
- Starting a ministry at your church
- Speaking up at the playground when the accessible equipment is being monopolized by children who don't have disabilities (and raising your voice when there IS NO accessible equipment)

- Volunteering to help with a local buddy walk or Down syndrome event
- Creating and/or designing merchandise for fundraising
- Creating an online platform to share your story
- Helping a nonprofit in the Down syndrome community with their gala

The list goes on and on and is not limited to any one way. The point, here, is to empower YOU, the reader, to utilize the tools you've collected in your tool belt for however long you've been living to help the community. Even if that means speaking up or sharing vulnerably in a doctor's appointment or when someone says something off base.

Recently I went to visit a specialist for a health issue I was experiencing. In the midst of our consultation, I brought up the fact that I had a son with Down syndrome and how my body has experienced a great deal of wear and tear since giving birth to him. I described how he will sometimes plop down and refuse to move and I have to sweep him up and carry him to the place we're going. When I was done explaining this, the specialist said, "So, I'm just curious, did you know your son had Down syndrome when you were pregnant?" I nodded. "What made you decide to keep the baby? I know most people in your situation would not."

Initially baffled and in shock from this overt question, I launched into a nervous monologue about how precious he is and the joy he brings to us. I talked about how I spend most days advocating online and try to spread the word in our local elementary schools and through public speaking around the country. I shared that I was scared, initially, but that Jed has crushed every preconceived notion I had and that there was nothing to fear. His life is worthy.

The specialist smiled and said, "That's awesome."

I went home angry. "How dare they ask me that!" I thought. "Where does anyone get off asking me questions like that?!" But as I thought it through a little more, I gained a bit more perspective. The fact is, most people in my situation DO abort. To be specific to the current time, 69% throughout the United States and 93% in New Jersey make a different choice than I did. So, from this person's point of view, I am parenting an endangered species.

While the question ignited feelings of confusion and anger, initially, I understood where the person was coming from and felt grateful for the chance to share our unique story. It may have been the first time this specialist had heard this point of view. I could have made the choice to find another option for this service, but I decided to keep going. I made the choice to keep showing up and speaking truth to this person. I wanted to SHOW them the beauty of Down syndrome through my words and my life with my precious Jed. People don't know what they don't know. Questions and words can seem offensive until you recognize that most people don't know any better. I certainly didn't before I had Jed. This was and IS an opportunity to spread the truth I had firsthand experienced about Down syndrome.

I share this story not to guilt or pressure someone into advocating when they don't feel equipped or energized to do so, but to share an alternate pathway.

Here is another example by a friend and leader in the Down syndrome community.

The Holy Pause of Advocating

By Cathy Daub, Co-Founder of Team Iron Will and Mom in the Down syndrome community

Advocacy for me is a work in progress. Online it's easy, I can write and rewrite my thoughts a hundred times before I post. I can run them by friends and not actually share until my response is filled with the utmost charity and heartfelt education. In person, that's not the case. I've had to teach myself to take a "holy pause." This has not been easy, but it's necessary if we want true change.

Most people are not malicious. They have just grown up in a world where stereotypes abound, where value is measured by production, and where no one has ever taught them how to see through the eyes of love. I remember a particularly hard moment. I called a local private school hoping Will could attend. The secretary was lovely until I said the words "Down syndrome" then she just stated plainly, "He cannot come to school here." I hung up and cried. Then I called back to speak with the principal. She confirmed proudly, "We've never had Down syndrome at our school." She said it the way you'd boast about never having had chicken pox. I got really upset. So upset she asked us to come visit (probably to make me be quiet). That was a mistake.

The entire meeting was spent showing me all the places in the school where Will would have a hard time—how he wouldn't' fit in. I left defeated and shot off an angry email to her and her superiors. I got crickets back. I'd changed nothing. My anger got the best of me and change doesn't really happen when it's fueled by anger. Passion yes. Anger. Not so much.

I've seen change when I'm willing to be part of the solution and not just upset by a broken system. Should Will have been welcomed at that school? Absolutely. But I could have approached it differently—with grace. It wasn't a school saying no to Will. It wasn't a church. It was a human consumed by the idea that keeping her school prestigious meant not letting in anyone who is different. If I had it to do again, I'm certain the outcome would be the same. He still wouldn't get in. That's a school that needs a true heart check and that takes time. But I think I could have left a greater impression if I had kept my cool. Advocacy is hard. It's exhausting. Especially when it's tied to a human being that you love with every fiber of your being. We only achieve a better world, when we help and encourage humans to be better people. And we can only do that when we start from a place of love ourselves. This Principal was fueled by misinformation and fear of the unknown. And the cure for that is education and love. Now when I advocate in person, I take that holy pause and remind myself that my grandmother was right—"you get a lot more flies with honey than you do with vinegar."

We all want to be extended grace and that starts when we learn how to extend it first, even when it's hard.

Sometimes advocating looks like walking into spaces and places with an unapologetic boldness and pride. Often our loved ones with Down syndrome do that on their own! This happened a couple of weeks ago when I went to a restaurant with my two sons. We sat at a table next to a man who looked like he'd never seen anyone with Down syndrome before. My inclination was to avoid the man's gaze and keep our distance. I could sense the man looking at us even after I sat with my back to him. I hopped up for maybe 20 seconds to get a cup of water for Jed and, when I returned, Jed was sitting at that man's table. Immediately I rushed to go get him and the man said, "it's ok! He's making a friend." I backed off and watched them interact and converse for at least three minutes. The man went from looking glum and grumpy to upbeat and almost childlike in his countenance.

This is the magic of Down syndrome. Jed has the uncanny ability to turn people's frowns upside down. And 99.9999% of the time, the people he interacts with seem to be better off than when he approached them. He has the gift of connection, and I'm honored to be a witness to it.

A Little Extra

It can be exhausting having to always feel like a living, breathing advocate. But when you turn that exhaustion on its ear and recognize the OPPORTUNITY we have to shed light on our loved ones, it becomes less like a burden and more like a gift. We GET to show up for our loved ones with Down syndrome. We GET to make a difference in the way others view the disability community. Slowly but surely, minds and hearts can change.

CHAPTER 11

Once the Bus Stops Coming

"I don't need easy. I just need possible."

—Bethany Hamilton

Go back with me to the bottom of my staircase in March of 2020, the day of my prenatal diagnosis. The fear invading those initial moments had the force of a tidal wave. I can *still* taste the terror as I sit here, thinking about it. But I can say wholeheartedly that the suffocating fear I felt had very little to do with the baby I was carrying. The movie in my mind was a self-imposed projection of my future, 20 or 30 years down the road. I envisioned a lack of freedom, resources, and support. I pictured an adult with Down syndrome who couldn't do anything for himself and a world that would only reject him at every corner. Sure, there would be therapists and services and resources to grab hold of but what on earth would I do when the bus stopped coming to take him to school?

Initially I felt guilty for these assumptions but, with time, I began to realize that I had no point of reference for anything different and that those feelings were shared by many parents in my situation. A fear of the future that has never been played out in real time, before your own eyes, is something that many parents in the Down syndrome community face. Especially in the early days.

So this chapter is dedicated to hearing the stories of parents who are much further down the path than I am. These parents have become mentors to me and many in the Down syndrome community because they openly share the highs and lows of the journey. Most importantly, they are living proof that there is hope for the future. Please, hold their words close to your heart.

Living in TODAY

By Holly Simon, Mother to a son with Down syndrome, Advocate

The title of this chapter, I'm told, is, Once the Bus Stops Coming. What a simple, profound sentence. I never understood the weight of those words—until now. Because it finally happened.

For 22 years, I lived in preparation for this moment. And yet, when it came, I wasn't ready. I had 22 years to prepare, and still, I failed.

When Nate was born 22 years ago, he was our fifth child. Like many of you already know, his arrival was met not with congratulations, but with sympathy. The doctors said they were sorry. Nate was robbed with the congratulations that my other four children received. He came into the world with a shadow of uncertainty cast by others' assumptions.

From the very beginning, Nate was medically fragile. The fear I carried felt endless—heavy and constant. I wore that fear like a cloak. But I didn't have time to fall apart. I had four other children who needed love, stability, and a mother who could keep it together. So, I put on a brave face, though my heart was often trembling behind it.

We heard so much nonsense in those early days. So many "cant's" and "wont's."

"He might not talk."

"He might not eat by mouth."

"He may never walk."

I remember those words vividly. And I remember wondering: How could they say such things before even knowing my son?

The day my husband told me Nate might not be able to have children, I literally threw the book I was reading about Down syndrome out the window. That moment marked the beginning of a lifelong lesson: no one can define our trajectory—not for Nate, not for any of us. So, we did what we knew best: we worked toward getting him healthy. Every single day. Because Nate deserved it. And because we loved him with every fiber of our being.

We had absolutely no idea what we were doing. But we asked questions and we stayed motivated. There was no way I was gonna allow my Nate to not succeed. He may have been doubted by medical professionals, neighbors, family, members, friends, but not by us. Not for one single second.

Once the worst of the medical emergencies began to fade—the constant doctor visits, the near-death experiences—we finally took a breath. And then school started.

I'll never forget when one of Nate's teachers asked if there was a manual on how to teach him. I laughed. "If you find one," I said, "please let me know. Because I need it too."

There's no manual. No road map. Just a beautiful baby boy who needed love, support, and a chance.

Are there days that I think I have failed? Absolutely! But I can safely say that I did the best that I could with what I knew. And I knew that with love anything was possible.

The best advice I ever received? "Enjoy the baby, not the diagnosis." I literally thought about that every day. I did not walk in a room with a child with down syndrome. He was my child. He was Nate.

Nate the great.

And that's what I tried to do. I just kept walking—literally, one foot in front of the other. Some days, I didn't think I could make it. And on those days, I wept quietly on the sofa. But the love never wavered. And the fact that Nate deserved more than the world expected from him—that became my fuel.

When Nate was around 10, I was diagnosed with breast cancer. That changed everything. For a while, I couldn't be the center of Nate's universe anymore. I had to focus on healing. But our village—our community—stepped up. They wrapped

(*continued*)

our family in love and support, so I could concentrate on surviving. And we made it.

After that chapter, we returned to school life. I still remember the day they told me Nate was "not educatable." Huh? This child—this curious, joyful, witty soul—they didn't think he could learn? Thankfully, there was one teacher who went to bat for us—and more importantly, for Nate. With her support, Nate blossomed. He became the class clown, the ladies' man, the charmer with a heart of gold. He had everyone wrapped around his finger in no time.

I never worried about tomorrow. I was too focused on making it through today.

And somehow, through all the noise and doubt, Nate built something beautiful. Today, at 22, Nate has done more than most people twice his age. He is a model. An actor. He played the lead in a feature film. He's a comedian, a singer, and a business owner. He's graced the pages of magazines and newspapers, been featured in commercials, and met more celebrities than I can count.

And the best part? He couldn't care less.

All Nate truly wants is to be included, accepted, appreciated, and loved.

And he is. Because Nate is the kind of soul who pulls people in. He teaches us how to see the world. How to slow down. How to feel. We never put parameters around Nate. We didn't define who he could be. We let him decide. And he chose to become someone extraordinary.

There's so much fear in this world. As a cancer survivor, I know how life can change in an instant. One phone call. One doctor's appointment. One heartbeat.

That realization changed me. It taught me not to live in tomorrow. Because today is the only guarantee we have.

All I've ever wanted was to help create the best version of a human being. If we could do that, I believed Nate's future would be dynamic. And it is. One day, he wants to be a barista. The next, a singer. Right now, he's the CEO of his own

Hawaiian shirt company—another beautiful, unexpected adventure.

Nate has magic in his veins. And it's a privilege to follow his lead through this life.

Am I afraid? Of course. Every day. But not for the reasons you might think. Nate is my fifth child—and honestly, the easiest one. He will find a job. He will make new friends. He will create a life that fulfills him. He already has.

My only real fear is that he won't be happy. But that's silly—because he IS happiness. He radiates it.

So I take it one day at a time. I try not to overthink. I allow goodness to unfold. Because it does—with Nate, it always does.

These 22 years have been an incredible, magical roller coaster ride. And though I have no idea what tomorrow will bring, I know this:

With God's grace, and with Nate's tenacity, it's going to be something extraordinary.

So even though there is no longer a bus. And school has ended, we will take each day and spread love and kindness. The way Nate does so effortlessly.

Our fears will never leave, but having a child with down syndrome turned out to be the least of my fears. Honestly, he turned out to be the biggest blessing of my life.

When the bus stopped coming for Holly, she could have been consumed by fears about the future. But she took the next right step with Nate guiding her and showing her what he could and *would* do. She's learning on the job that there is hope and light and possibility for her son. There is hope and light for the whole Down syndrome community and for the entire world that will receive our community. There are challenges and massive question marks along the way but wouldn't that be true for any parent and child?

That is real life.

Real life is worth living and also full of challenges and uncharted waters. When that bus stops coming and the graduation has come and go, what does the everyday humdrum look like?

Where Does the Graduation Cap Land?

By Amy Julia Becker, Author, Advocate, Speaker, Podcast Host and Mother in the Down syndrome community

The day of high school graduation is a little scary for most parents. I don't think I'm alone in saying that it's a lot scary for parents of teenagers with Down syndrome. I heard from other parents that once Penny had finished high school, she would "fall off a cliff" when it came to support, services, and community. Loneliness and boredom both seemed inevitable.

But we live in a school district with more opportunities than most, and our daughter Penny was invited to apply to a local college program. She joined a group of other students with Intellectual Developmental Disabilities (IDD) in the fall of 2024, with transportation and tuition provided by our town. It wasn't perfect, but it was good enough. (See the Self Advocate Chapter for her daughter, Penny's description of the program.)

Still, loneliness and boredom haunted us during the eight hours each day after school, plus 48 hours of the weekend. Back in high school, Penny participated in clubs, attended dances, and became a regular fan at sporting events. At her new college, with students from all over the state and no invitations to get involved in clubs or sports, she was alone every afternoon. She spent hours in front of Netflix, TikTok, and Instagram.

Eventually, we implemented some rules around screens. Penny started walking on the treadmill and reading books in the afternoon. We began to pursue other activities in our community. Now, she spends time once or twice a week with people from church, attends two ballet classes, and bowls with the Special Olympics. She's making friends at school. We are building a life with connections to our community step by step.

The future feels both promising and daunting. Penny wants to pursue a residential college program, and we will try to help her find a summer job. Neither of those will come easily. Still, the world of exclusion is changing day by day, as families like ours insist on showing up and contributing to our communities. Step by step, I believe we can be a part of creating a world of belonging.

The future feeling, both *promising and daunting*, is a sentiment I can get behind. Reading through these stories, I am simultaneously struck by excitement and uncertainty and I've come to learn that it is A-OK. We, as parents of children with Down syndrome, are allowed to feel two things at once. There is room for the good and the hard together. There is a whole lot of grey on this journey.

But there is also an abundance of color. There are a myriad of experiences yet to be had. No two journeys will look the same. Mia, who you will hear from directly in Chapter 14, is on a path that I didn't think existed in the Down syndrome community until I heard her sing right in front of me a few years ago. Her mother, Natalie describes the twists and turns of their path with beautiful perspective.

Singing Through Life

By Natalie Saenz—Mother, Advocate

When Mia was born, I remember feeling like I got pushed into a marathon that I didn't choose and wasn't ready or trained to run, and I couldn't stop running. Those early years were overwhelming, full of anxieties and questions, and I often felt like I couldn't slow down enough to simply enjoy

(*continued*)

my baby the way other moms seemed to. Looking back now, I see that those years were the foundation for my strength, courage, and a new different vision of life. Those moments of pain and worry I carried into IEP meetings, medical appointments, or testing sessions were not weakness; it was love. A love so deep that it pressed on my heart and reshaped me into someone who had to rise to meet it. God gave me that love through Mia, and with it came a new purpose: to learn, to teach, to advocate, and to grow into the mom she needed me to be.

Every stage of Mia's life has brought so much richness and own lessons. And while some people like to say that you should live in the present (and I agree and really try hard to), I have to keep an eye in the future. With Mia's elementary school years, I was already thinking about middle school. During middle school, I was already looking toward high school. Now that Mia is in high school, I'm already preparing for college. With Mia, we've always needed to think two or three steps ahead; not because she can't keep up, but because the systems around her often aren't ready for her. And so, as parents, we imagine and we plan. If the supports don't exist, we dream, we imagine and we go out there and create them. Through it all, Mia has been involved in these decisions, because they are her life and her future. That, too, has shaped me and has taught me that advocacy isn't about speaking for her, but speaking with her until others learn to truly listen.

Along the way, I've discovered something else: most people don't intend harm. When teachers or professionals underestimate Mia, it is not usually from bad intentions . . . it's from not knowing. They, too, have to be taught. That realization shifted my fight into something more sustainable: advocating with love. That advocacy that teaches, invites, and opens doors. And in the middle of all of this, I find so much joy in simply being her mom. I love watching her grow into herself, becoming a strong, kind, and talented teenager with dreams that are entirely her own. There is nothing more beautiful than experiencing love through this lens. It has changed me forever.

Watching dreams come true with our children can be a wondrous experience. Families should have the freedom to imagine the possibilities! But often, the monotony of the day-in and day-out checklists can bog us down with weight. Heather explains a bit about those feelings, here.

The Practicalities of Life

By Heather Wenzel, Mother, Advocate

Life after high school has been a major adjustment for Luke and for me as his parent. In school, everything was structured and entitlements were guaranteed until he aged out at 21. Once he transitioned to adult services, it felt like we fell off a cliff. Now, the Division of Developmental Disabilities (DDD) provides him with a budget based on the NJCAT assessment, and we work with a support coordinator to process the services we choose for him—like classes at the community college, drum lessons, and transportation. But I quickly learned that the support coordinator's role is more about paperwork than actual support. Nearly 40% of Luke's budget is tied up in transportation, leaving less flexibility than I expected. On top of that, I'm responsible for approving invoices, completing training, and making sure his days are meaningful and full. It's not difficult work, but it is constant, and the weight of it falls on me every day.

Right now, Luke attends three pre-college classes at our local community college, and he works two mornings a week at a senior center, helping residents with their groceries. He loves the structure, and I believe he could handle more, though opportunities are not easy to secure. I've pursued possible cafeteria work with the district, but communication has been frustrating, and even working with DVRS hasn't yielded much hope. We are largely on our own. That's overwhelming, especially when I think about how much Luke misses his school friends and the steady rhythm of unified sports. And how much was done for us while he was there.

(*continued*)

We hosted a gathering recently with his friends and their parents, and it reminded me how valuable it is to stay connected with others who understand this stage. The advice I would pass along to parents still in the school system is to learn as much as you can before your child turns 21. Attend workshops and take notes even if the topics don't feel relevant yet. You'll likely need that information sooner than you think. And most importantly, keep building community—because none of us should have to navigate this boat alone.

No one *should* have to walk this path alone, and finding a solid community can ensure that we don't! All throughout these pages, we've been learning and *will* learn about resources, programs, sites, individuals, and everything in between that are bursting from every corner of the Down syndrome world. Liz Plachta has been a major force for good in this space since her daughter Ruby was born.

A Life of Higher Education

By Liz Plachta, Founder of Ruby's Rainbow and Mother in the Down syndrome community

I always joke that Ruby came "early, tiny and rockin' an extra chromosome." They told me she had Down syndrome before I got to hold her for the very first time, and if I am being honest—I didn't know anything about Down syndrome at the time of her birth. We got to take her home after about three weeks in the NICU, and the only thing I really knew about Down syndrome was what Ruby showed me: she was strong. She was capable. She was determined. She was smart. And she was adorable. But of course as a new mama on this unexpected journey, I wanted to know EVERYTHING there was to know about Down syndrome. . .so when I got home, I went out to the library and checked out literally every book I could find. But you know what? None of the books depicted this perfect little human that

I watched grow every day. This perfect little human who worked so incredibly hard every single day to be the best lil' version of herself she could be. None of them talked about all the amazing things she was going to do with her life, the possibilities or even the opportunities that might be available.

She wasn't even a few months old, but she had already taught me so much about resilience, acceptance, and patience. I knew there was more. I knew she was more, was better, and was capable of amazing things . . . things that books and society weren't telling me about. So it was at that moment I shut the books and decided to let her guide me and show me the way. Ruby's future was not going to be determined by some outdated book. I was going to do my best to give her all the right support to help her grow and thrive . . . but only she would determine how high she would fly.

The moment I held Ruby for the first time, I just knew I had to do something to show the world what I saw in my daughter. It was almost like a lightning bolt shot out from her heart to mine, and I had this insane bright light and energy waiting to burst out of my soul. After getting her home and settled, I really started wondering about the possibilities for her future. I figured I could control the "now" by being sure she got the therapies she needed, working with her, including her in every aspect of our life . . . but what about the future? I knew I wanted Ruby to have all the same opportunities her big sister may have someday . . . including college.

I remember so clearly coming to my husband when Ruby was about six months old and saying, "I think I want to help someone with Down syndrome go to college." We didn't even know if people with Down syndrome were going to college, but I knew in my heart Ruby was capable of amazing things, and I wanted to help someone rockin' it—just like her—go and do amazing things. This is when Ruby's Rainbow was born. Well, actually, the organization was likely born the first time I held Ruby . . . I just didn't know it then. Her spirit and determination inspired us to start a nonprofit and stand up and shout

(*continued*)

as loud as we can that people with Down syndrome are amazing, capable, and worthy!

Since her birth, we have been about to grant millions of dollars in college scholarships to hundreds of people rockin' that extra chromosome! And showing the world the value and worth of people rockin' it like my daughter has also proven to be another one of my life's missions. Because we all deserve the opportunity to be the best we can be and to have people believe you are worthy of it all!

Ruby's Rainbow is an incredibly powerful example of possibility. The sky is the limit for individuals with Down syndrome, and no one should ever be held back, discriminated against, or left behind. Presuming competence is the way to go and the stark contrast between what once *was* and what now *can be* is staggering and encouraging.

However, a path to college may not be the story of every individual in this community. Higher education isn't the path for every person in the typical community, either. Each person has unique gifts and abilities that can be seen, utilized, and tapped into in a variety of ways. Variety is the spice of life, and it's important to not get caught in the comparison trap once again.

Here are some thoughts from a mom whose 22-year-old son has Down syndrome. Your experience may (and probably will) vary!

The Sweetness of Life

By Sue Spies, Mother and Advocate in the Down syndrome community

We have all seen videos and heard stories about people with Down Syndrome exceeding expectations, knocking down barriers, and excelling to a degree that rivals, or even surpasses, their typical peers. This is wonderful, inspirational, and a dynamic that is found in the "typical" community as well. There are always superstars. But, it is important to remember that there are so many others in any community that live lives in the realm of the ordinary. In those ordinary lives, accomplishments may be less extraordinary but no less worthy of celebration. We celebrate milestones that may come later, or stall at a lower level of achievement, but we celebrate nonetheless, with joy and satisfaction, appreciating the work and persistence necessary to accomplish these goals.

The future is brighter for our kids now than if they had been born 50–60 years ago. Thankfully, medical advances have given our kids a real shot at a long and healthy life. While there is still much need for greater acceptance and inclusion, there are programs that provide opportunities for social, spiritual, educational, artistic, athletic, and vocational development after graduation. Discovering these opportunities was very encouraging to us as parents. Our son takes part in a number of programs and activities which he enjoys and which broaden his life experiences and skills. We have been able to tap into opportunities that give him a full life.

As parents, especially as a Mom, I try to keep both feet planted in the present, while preparing for the future for our son. My husband and I have raised our kids with the understanding that no matter how deeply we love our kids, Jesus loves them even more. This is a great comfort when I can stay grounded in that fact. But, I must confess, I often find myself living in the "what ifs" regarding the day to day of our son's future once we are gone. We are blessed to know that he will always have a loving, supportive advocate and protector in his sister. They love each other deeply. But, because our son deals with severe apraxia of speech, it is difficult for him to communicate clearly, despite various tools and techniques to support his communication. Will others put in the time and effort to understand his communication? Will he feel heard? Will he be understood? God willing, people will not take advantage of him. I pray for patient, caring people to be in his life, throughout his life.

(*continued*)

In addition to having an extra chromosome, our kids often have something extra. There can be a sweetness to our kids that, gratefully, doesn't seem to fade with age, at least in our case. We were on a very long vacation recently that allowed us to see many wonderful sites—mountains, waterfalls, prairies, glaciers, wildlife, museums, and more. Far into the trip, while we were driving from one scenic overlook to the next, our son reached from behind, hugged me and said "thank you."

On this same trip, we were in a gift shop. I was checking out; he was off looking at something. A couple of minutes later, I saw him at a different cashier. He had a necklace on the counter and was pulling out money from his wallet (some ones). The cashier smiled and looked at me. "Hey bud," I said, "we aren't getting that today, ok?" He put his money back. The necklace was for a girl he has liked for years. They were friends from earlier years in school, but they have gone their separate ways. He still talks about her in the sweetest way. He is a grown man, but in some ways he has retained the sweetness he has always had.

Our kids have many opportunities now, depending on ability and interest. Many opportunities require research on the part of the parent/caregiver, but that is something we all, as parents, have been doing since day one.

We are so proud of the young man our son has become. We have, of course, taught him. But he has taught us, as well. He has been a gift to us, filling a hole in our family we didn't know we had. But God did. So, we walk with him as we always have. Now through adulthood, trusting the One that knew him before we did. Grateful to Him, for him.

A Little Extra

Before Jed was born, I had no prior knowledge about individuals with Down syndrome attending college or even graduating High School. The preconceived notions and biases I possessed without even knowing I had them is absolutely staggering to think about in this current iteration of myself. It's possible that many of us have these types of leanings and aren't even aware of that fact.

A few months into Jed's life, I became very active on Instagram and started learning about individuals with Down syndrome reading, writing, working, graduating high school, pursuing higher education, and starting their own businesses. I discovered models, actors, singers, artists, and scholars with an extra chromosome that I had never heard of nor dreamed of as a possibility for this particular population. But there is a whole world of stories yet to be written. Regardless of *how* or *what* an individual with Down syndrome accomplishes in their life, they have innate value, worth, and beauty.

CHAPTER 12

What About the Future?

> *"You do not have to see the whole staircase, you just have to take the first step."*
>
> —Martin Luther King Jr.

Most parents in the disability community have some pretty strong emotions and common worries attached to what the future may or may not bring for their child. The path is often filled with unpredictable twists and turns and, no matter how much you've planned for the future of your children, disability parenting can feel like a constantly moving target. Some of the questions that can pop up at any given moment include:

- What happens to my child when I die?
- How will they be financially stable?
- What if too much falls on siblings?
- How can I keep them safe?
- What about long-term care?
- What if they are discriminated against?
- What if they don't have equal opportunity?
- What about their social, emotional, physical, spiritual development?
- Where do I even begin to plan for the "What ifs?"

I've experienced these worries and spiraling thoughts many times, particularly in the beginning of Jed's life. My son had barely entered the world, and I was worrying about what would happen to him when I was no longer here. I felt a strong sense of overwhelm when I began to explore avenues for the future because there can be a lot of hypotheticals and contingency plans. Sometimes it feels like you're getting ahead of yourself and other times it feels like you're behind the eight ball. How on earth can someone find a happy medium?

In an article entitled, "How Parents Can Build A Support System For Adult Children With Disabilities," Jenny Price reminds us that,

> "One in four Americans have some kind of disability. Adults with disabilities are living much longer than in the past, which means their aging parents must plan for the likelihood that their dependent children will outlive them."[1]

Co-Founder of CaringTide (keep reading for more about this organization, later in the chapter), Jennie Dopp, is an ideal example of someone who is equipped to help along this path. When it comes to protecting Financial Assistance Assets, Jennie advises that caregivers should consult with an estate planning attorney who specializes in Disability Planning. Caregivers should avoid probate and death taxes. Typical estate planning for parents of children with disabilities will include: a revocable family trust, wills for both parents, Powers of Attorney for both parents, Medical Directives for both parents, and a third-party supplemental needs trust (or third-party special needs trust) for the loved one with a disability.

Jennie is a trusted friend and professional advisor to many families like mine and is a wealth of knowledge when it comes to planning for the future. In a recent conversation, she shared some tips that I'm relaying here for the benefit of all who may need it!

First, any amount of money can be put into a special needs trust and the funds in the trust don't count when determining eligibility for government benefits. If parental assets are left directly to a loved one with a disability, they could be a countable asset. There is no need to disown your loved one. With proper estate planning, you can pass your assets to your loved one and save for their future.

It's important to start early! Set up a third-party supplemental needs (third-party special needs) trust. The age doesn't necessarily matter when it comes to setting up the trust but it's important that you do this as soon as possible. Your loved one with a disability should not have countable assets in their name because that could prevent them from being eligible for public benefits like Social Security and Medicaid. If you were to pass away, your loved one could inherit your assets and therefore not be eligible for benefits. Work with a qualified Elder Law attorney or someone who is experienced in Special Needs Trusts to help you with the drafting of the estate planning documents.

Be sure to follow the rules and ensure that your child receives SSI benefits, money from the trust cannot be the primary source of income used for rent. Use your loved ones SSI first for basic needs. You can then use the trust money or funds from your loved one's ABLE Account to supplement their needs.

The trustee you choose should be someone who can manage your child's affairs after you are gone. You can choose one person who oversees all aspects of life (financial, care coordination, housing, benefit management, etc.), or you can choose several people to fill individual roles. Choosing someone to be the financial trustee should be someone who can make responsible financial decisions, follow the rules and laws associated with special needs trusts, and be able to invest the funds within the trust as well as filing the taxes on the trust. Some families may choose a family member; others may choose a corporate trustee or opt for a pooled trust. Every family's situation is different, and your attorney can help to guide you based on your circumstances.

And for those, like me, who had zero knowledge of ABLE Accounts before Jed was born, here is what Jennie says:

> "An ABLE Account is a specific type of savings account for a person with a qualifying disability. Medicaid and Social Security do not look at the money in an ABLE account when considering asset eligibility. As of 2026, anyone can contribute up to $19,000 per year and if the individual is working, they can contribute an additional $15,560 per year. However, if the person is receiving SSI, once the ABLE reaches $100,000, SSI will

be paused until the account is spent down. Funds can also be transferred from an SSI Representative Payee Account to an ABLE and from a Third Party Trust to an ABLE. Some states do require Medicaid Re+covery, so it is important to understand how to leverage an ABLE into your planning strategy.

"The plans you make should address your child's wishes and you should involve your child in the process to the extent possible. It is also important to not plan in a silo. Yes, we can set aside money, and we can create a trust. However, while important, those are just two aspects of planning. We also want to discuss our plan with other family members or friends who may potentially be involved. While we all hope to live one day longer than our child, life is unpredictable. Putting a plan in place is something we can do to provide and advocate now and for when we are no longer here."

Let it be noted during this chapter that, *I, Misty Coy Snyder, am not an attorney or financial planner. This is just general education and guidance that you can use as you work with your own planning professionals.*

As I stated in the Introduction of the book, I am a connector of many people with a variety of experiences and expertise. One of my favorite parts of advocating on a daily basis for the Down syndrome community is getting connected with individuals, organizations, and businesses that DO specialize in these matters and help families like mine. For a little over a year, I've had the privilege of co-hosting (alongside Team Iron Will in Chapter 16) FREE, empowering webinars that offer invaluable resources. From Speech to Oral Hygiene, Medical Advocacy to Self Care for Caregivers, and everything in between, these webinars bring to light the vast resources in the disability community. CaringTide is an example of one such organization.

CaringTide provides long-term planning for the whole family in addition to your loved one with Down syndrome. The founders take pride in combining personal experience with professional expertise. Legal Professionals, Certified Financial Planners, Tax Specialists, and Chartered Special Needs Consultants come together to assure families will receive professional guidance and direction, customized to their unique needs. Their team members are genuinely passionate advocates for the disability community and bring personal insight and empathy. The beauty of working with an organization like CaringTide is knowing that the founders are not leading blindly. They have firsthand experience that gives them the ability to empathize and guide.

I sat down with Brady Murray and Jennie Dopp, the Co-Founders of the organization and the following is what they had to share about their mission.

When Professional Experience Gets Personal

By Brady Murray, Certified Financial Planner (CFP), Advocate and Dad in the Down syndrome community

When I received the birth diagnosis of Down syndrome for my son, Nash, it rocked my world and was a terrifying experience, initially. There was a great deal of grief and sorrow that felt heavy on my shoulders. As I began to spend time with my son and was able to experience Down syndrome, however, all of those things started to go away, and it just kept getting better. When he was learning to walk and talk and growing so much, I thought, "It can't get better than this." When he was 12 and he started puberty and all the pure innocence of a human soul feeling all the things the body feels during that time I thought, "It can't get better than this!" It has been among my life's greatest blessings. Our journey has not been without its challenges, however and I'm sure there will be curve balls that will be thrown at us in the future that have the potential to be difficult and heart-wrenching.

I've worked as a certified financial planner for my entire career, over 20 years now, and I pride myself on putting forth a solid plan for my own family. Early on in our journey, we had a special needs trust set up and we put funding mechanisms in place to be able to take care of that trust. To me, it seemed like all the details were covered. However, about five years ago, our family was going through an intense and rocky time. We were

(*continued*)

parenting Nash, who has Down syndrome along with our adopted son with Down syndrome, Cooper. We had recently brought in two little girls that had dealt with trauma, and we were in the process of fostering them and later, adopting them. One of our other sons had a newly identified 22q gene deletion diagnosis and all of those factors were starting to converge at the same time.

I'll never forget planning a birthday party for our son, Nash, and my wife and I were talking about the future. I remember clearly hearing Andrea say, "Honey I love that you are such a visionary and looking into the future, but I really need help right now. I need help today in navigating through all the things we are faced with in the present. I've heard I'm supposed to get these kids on this waiver wait list, but I have no idea how to do that! I'm worried about what happens when the school bus stops coming to pick up Nash. What will that look like for him and for Cooper, then?"

All of these questions were flooding into my mind and most of them were pressing for our current season of life. And so, as a dad and spouse who adores my family, I wanted to do whatever I could to help. I started to look throughout my state for resources or a team. I desperately craved a guide that could take some of the weight off my shoulders on this pack that Andrea and I were carrying. More than anything, I hoped for someone to not just point in which direction we should go up the mountain but also walk up the mountain with us. Someone to help steer us through the peaks and valleys and conquer what seemed like an insurmountable mountain. I couldn't find anybody in my state, so I started looking nationwide.

In that search I found that, similar to my state search, there were wonderful people that specialized in certain things but there was nobody that could be my Sherpa. That's when I realized that this was a service that was and IS desperately needed in our community. So, I thought, "Let's go build it!"

And build it they did. He and Jennie Dopp (who we heard from earlier in the chapter) set out to provide a safe space with a plethora of resources and guidance for families in the disabilities community. Jennie does not have a child with Down syndrome, but she has a journey that has been challenging to navigate its own right. Here is some of her experience.

The Mission and Purpose of CaringTide

By Jennie Dopp, Chartered Special Needs Consultant (ChSNC) and Mom in the disability community

Five months in utero, Jackson was diagnosed with a rare brain anomaly and enlarged ventricles. At the time, we just thought it was going to be delayed development. We didn't know what we were dealing with and how best to help him, other than just regular therapies. With every step, we were not only trying to figure out our path forward but also struggling with things like insurance coverage. Nothing was approved because of the lack of a diagnosis.

In addition to needing a treatment path and therapy, we lacked a support system within the disability community. As we floundered and tried to connect with other parents, oftentimes, well-intentioned people would say, "Oh, don't worry, my child does that, too. . ." But it was in no way the same. Oh, how we wished someone could guide us and show us the way.

The purpose of CaringTide is to provide every family in America affected by disabilities with support as they plan for the future. We want families to know they're not alone, and CaringTide is there to help. We will show you the path forward and guide you along the way. As we help families navigate life care planning for the future, we know every family's situation and plan will be different. Acknowledging that everyone's story is different is crucial. Our loved ones are unique, and so should be our planning. We want to be sure to plan for the basics, like legal and estate planning. However, we also want to plan for

(*continued*)

our family's unique needs. We all just have this one, present day, guaranteed.

Try not to be overwhelmed and focus on what is the one thing you can do today. This path of planning for the future can definitely feel like a lot, and it's okay to acknowledge that and give yourself grace. All we can do is put one foot in front of the other and take the next right step. In addition to CaringTide, find people who can meet you where you are. As Mr. Rogers once said, "Find the helpers." There's somebody who has walked this path before you. Let them guide you.

Conversely, we can't just ignore this and bury our heads in the sand, either. There are actual tasks we, as caregivers, have to do, whether it's the IEP, opening an Able Account, or establishing a Third-Party Supplemental (Special Needs) Trust. We need to do the next right thing to advocate and protect our loved ones. One of the most common fears we hear is, "What will happen when I'm no longer here?" It's a valid concern.

At CaringTide, we help families navigate this process and establish a lifecare plan for your loved one and your family. Through our planning process, you will have a roadmap for helping your loved one live their best life, now and in the future. We also work with the self-advocate to empower them to live their best life with the person-centered planning we do with families. There is no one-size-fits-all plan, and that is why we encourage customized plans.

A Little Extra

This piece of the journey can be so difficult for many of us. We want to remain present and fully stand where our feet are planted, but we recognize that there ARE things to think about for the future. It doesn't have to be done all at once, but it is important to acknowledge that proper planning is necessary. Utilizing a one-on-one guide like Jennie or Brady at Caring Tide can take the immense pressure and overwhelm off your shoulders so you can hike up that mountain with some awareness of the beautiful view around you.

CHAPTER 13

A Word to Friends and Family

"Support and love are the pillars of strength."

—Anonymous

It's a given that there is often a struggle for parents to come to terms with a Down syndrome diagnosis. It's not really something most people expect or even consider as a possibility when embarking on their parenting journeys. Thanks to many individuals in the disability space and the organizations mentioned in this book (and many more), there are resources and pathways for expecting parents as they piece things together.

But where does that leave the friends and family of those parents? How do *they* respond to those unexpected words . . . Down syndrome? Questions may arise such as:

- What should I say?
- Do I say anything at all?
- Is, "I'm so sorry" for a moment like this?
- Should I leave them alone as they process and grieve the baby they thought they were having?
- How can I best support them?

All of these are valid questions and concerns that speak to your desire to want the best for the expecting parents—your friend or family member. As you consider the unique circumstance you find yourself in, here are some DOs and DO NOTs that offer some guidelines.

Dos and Do Nots

- *What should I say?*

There is no perfect thing to say but here are a couple of options:

"I know this is unexpected news and I want you to know that I am here for you. I support you. You don't have to walk this path alone."

"Your baby was loved before we knew of the Down syndrome diagnosis and the baby is still loved, every bit as much."

"It's ok to grieve the baby you thought you were having. There is no shame in that. It won't always feel this way and your baby is beloved just as they are! I will be here to walk alongside you as you navigate this."

There are many variations of statements like these but the important thing is to remain open, supportive and kind. Your loved one is experiencing a whirlwind of emotion and you can be supportive by letting them experience the worries and fears they have in real time. Rushing to rid themselves of their genuine feelings will not lead to healing. It will lead to repressing and hiding. Encourage your loved one to be open and honest and offer a safe place for them.

- *Do I say anything at all?*

Yes. Please say something. You can even say, "I don't know what to say at this moment. But I love you and I'm here for you." Resist the urge to run from the person or avoid them. After a diagnosis, parents need support and ghosting them is quite possibly the most detrimental thing you can do.

- *Should I say, "I'm sorry" for a moment like this?*

No. Please do not say, "I'm sorry." It can be difficult to keep those words from coming out because you see tears streaming down and worries on their face. But hearing someone you love say they are sorry for a baby that belongs to them is one of the most painful things to experience. Even if it is meant well. In lieu of saying a blanket, "I'm sorry," consider saying something like:

> "I'm sorry for what you're going through right now and I am here for you. I celebrate this new life, your sweet baby, and I am here to help. I'm not going anywhere."
>
> OR
>
> "I know you weren't expecting this and I know this comes as a shock or surprise. I'm here for it. I'm here for you and your baby. I love you. You WILL make it through this. We will learn together."

- *Should I leave them alone as they process and grieve the baby they thought they were having?*

Let the parents lead the way. A great deal of people who have a new diagnosis don't know what they need. One moment they may want to be alone and the next moment they may really want people to sit with them and listen to what they are processing. Rather than assuming they want to be left alone, do your best to serve and love them. You can do this by:

- **Picking up groceries and leaving them on the doorstep.** If you aren't sure what they need or want, pick up toilet paper and paper towels! People always need that. If the baby is born, pick up wipes, formula, diapers, etc. Even if they indicate they don't want people around, they still need help and basic necessities. A DoorDash Gift card can be helpful, too.
- **Sending a card in the mail.** It cannot be overstated that your friend or loved one needs your support and care. They need glimmers of hope and light throughout their day. Calling, texting, and emailing work, too, but a card shows extra effort and thoughtfulness.

- **Offer to babysit the other children.** When the diagnosis comes, it can be hard for parents to know how to properly care for and engage with the other children in their home. Offer to help with that, even if means staying in their house while they go for a walk or taking their children out for ice cream.

- *How can I best support them?*

You know your friend and loved one, best. Again, there is no "one-size-fits-all" remedy for a situation like this. But there are definitely ways to show your support that will encourage and uplift them as they process. I will never forget receiving a care package from my friend Tia. She wrote the sweetest card, had some goodies inside, and sent a really funny card game that my husband and I played together. Since my diagnosis came in the heart of COVID, there weren't many things we could do for fun. It meant the world to receive a gift that made me laugh AND cry. She knew me and loved me SO well through that thoughtful gesture.

These are some ideas to support a loved one who just received a diagnosis.

How to Help a Friend

But what about that friend or family member who is grieving or terrified, themselves? How do they process through this unexpected turn of events? I recently had a grandparent reach out to me through my platform "Happiness is Down syndrome" on Instagram. I could tell they were very hesitant to share or reveal too much of what they were feeling. But after some back and forth, they eventually typed, "I'm really scared. I feel like this is going to change the dynamic of our family and I'm worried. How can I help my daughter rejoice and accept if I'm unable to do the same?"

The question stopped me in my tracks. My family and friends had been so accepting and gracious when they spoke to me that I hadn't even considered that they might be struggling internally. I hadn't thought of the grandparents, aunts/uncles, and even husbands or wives, themselves who are grieving in various degrees and don't have an outlet to share or voice their worries. While I can't speak to these experiences directly, I decided to reach out to friends and allies of the Down syndrome community who might be able to shed light on the feelings that can arise to those on the periphery.

One of the first calls I made after finding out Jed would most likely have Down syndrome was to my once boss, turned close friend, brother from another mother, Robert Tichio. He describes his experience hearing the news of my prenatal diagnosis in, Doomscrolling to Discovery.

Doomscrolling to Discovery

By Robert Tichio, An Adopted Member of the Down syndrome community

I remember exactly where I was when I learned the news. It was March 6, 2020, and it was 4:43 pm. I was sitting in my kitchen, on Twitter, "doomscrolling" over the news flow in the early days of what would become COVID-19. Just a half hour earlier, at 3:42 pm, Elon Musk would tweet "The coronavirus panic is dumb," words of unbridled confidence from the world's wealthiest man that would age about as well as a three-month old gallon of milk would at room temperature. If I close my eyes right now, I can see the dirty spoon with Haagen Daz vanilla ice cream sitting on the kitchen counter, the crumbs from a half-eaten slice of lemon pound cake from Starbucks about four inches away. The text from my beloved sister from another mother, Misty, came with no forewarning and landed with the kind of impact you'd expect it to. It began I don't know how to type this. I just got a call from the doctor.

The hours, days, weeks, and months thereafter were a slurry of memories as the world quite literally stopped. My heart and head remained out of my body 25 miles away from my home in New York City to where Misty, her husband, and their precious son Clay lived. I remember the agony she experienced with news that defined the "unknown," but I just as clearly remember the conviction with which she showed the world in even the earliest moments following receipt of the news that she would embrace this path God had laid before her, and do it with the

(*continued*)

steely resolve that has defined every ounce of who she is. Misty and I were bound as forever soulmates when she became nanny to my newborn over 17 years ago, and while our professional relationship has long ceased, we became the sort of friends that you not only wish for but that only with the passage of time do you know you need.

Our lives have gone through trials and tribulations—disappointments, divorces—but joy-filled moments and celebrations, too. Later that March night back in 2020, I was in the shower, unable to move my mind past her news, and God came upon my heart like a thunderbolt with Jeremiah 29:11, "'For I know the plans I have for you,' declares the Lord." Both children of the church, products of youth groups and Bible summer camps, Misty and I always found comfort in Jesus and the Word our God left for us as the owner's manual of our lives. She replied with an "Amen," and the night continued.

I now sit in reflection over five . . . FIVE . . . years later, and I have a different set of emotions when I think of Misty and her walk over the last five years. You see, I know Jed—her (our!) beloved treasure of a blessing for this broken world—and I hadn't known him in March 2020. I feel almost embarrassed for the depths of sadness I felt when I learned of her in-utero diagnosis of Downs Syndrome, but I now know my sadness was to be the seed of the great gift God would bestow upon *me*.

My sadness was rooted in two emotions, equally yoked: first the fear of the unknown, and second the anger of the robbing of innocence for my dearest friend. You have to understand that Misty had not lived a charmed life—rather, hers was a hardscrabble existence of stretched finances growing up, addiction as a young adult, and heartbreak and loss in her first marriage. When she had shared months earlier the news of her second pregnancy, I really felt that God was finally giving her the life she deserved. I actually now believe that He *did* in fact give her the life she deserved, and which we *all* deserved: He gifted the universe with Jed's beauty and ethos. I didn't know I needed Jed. But I did.

Armed with two Ivy League degrees, I have been taught more by my beloved Misty through her eyes for Jed than any instructor or class has ever. In the last five years, she has been an ambassador in this world. An ambassador of kindness, acceptance, gratitude, understanding, and appreciation. Misty is an artist by constitution and educational training, and her art in this world is now in showing the unmatched beauty in a corner of our humanity that the world doesn't easily see. She is a self-declared "Momma Bear," a fierce protector and vocal advocate for the defeated or marginalized, and she is my modern-day clarion for both inclusivity and a "stop, look, and listen to the beauty before your eyes" worldview that I now marshal with frequency and ardent enthusiasm. I affectionately tell people that to know Misty is to live within a "compassion blast zone."

I look to my own two children, ages 15 and 18, who were entrusted in her care in their early years, and see how they have come to know empathy and inclusivity because of Misty and Jed. Through that alone, I know that God's purpose is fulfilled with resplendent and amplified intention on the daily. In the end, Down Syndrome has blessed my life. Those are words that five years ago I would not be able to say, but now I can and do with pride and love.

Robert, a brilliant man of great success, has changed for the better because of Down syndrome. By his own admission, he would not and COULD NOT have said that before his brush with Trisomy 21 in the form of my beautiful boy. I remember hearing the shock and worry in his voice when I shared the news. He offered to drive a far distance to come be with my husband and me, which spoke to how seriously he took this situation. Knowing how differently he feels now is a dynamic example of the power of having someone with Down syndrome in your life. While I can't take credit for his vast accomplishments in other realms, I most certainly take pride and joy in the fact that my little boy has impacted him for the better. And he's not the only one.

Cami Nelson, a professional photographer who uses her artistry to photograph and capture moments of individuals with Down syndrome and other disabilities, describes an impactful moment with a fellow professional that helped her hone in on her purpose.

Finding Purpose and Passion in Art

By Cami Nelson, Professional Photographer and ally to the Down syndrome community

Although I don't believe it was an accident, I often say that I stumbled into the Down syndrome community in 2021—completely unaware of how profoundly it would change my life. I could talk all day about how these beautiful individuals bring joy to my heart, a smile to my face, energy to my sessions, and purpose to my work. But let me share one story that made it clear to me that this is the best place in the world to be.

Last year, I was sitting at a wedding reception for a friend. By chance, I found myself next to another photographer, and naturally, I asked him about his work. He told me he was a celebrity portrait photographer. As we scrolled through his gallery, familiar faces of well-known stars flashed across his screen. I'll admit, I felt a twinge of jealousy. It seemed like he had "made it" as a photographer, while I—after 21 years behind the camera—had just shifted the entire direction of my business into the disability community, essentially starting over.

When it was my turn, I showed him portraits of individuals with disabilities. I spoke about their love and openness, how these sessions filled me up in ways I'd never expected, and even shed a few tears as I shared my journey into the Down syndrome community. As I spoke, I could feel my heart warming and expanding inside me. I knew, yet again, that this was where I was meant to be—where I wanted to be. When I finished sharing, I waited. I wondered what this artist—someone who, by the world's standards, had achieved real success—would think of my work, my offering, my heart.

He paused just long enough for me to start to feel a bit uneasy. Then he sighed deeply and said, "I bet these images really mean something to your clients. The celebrities I photograph come in and stand there like it's just another day at the office. I don't mean anything to them. But I see joy and beauty in these images. They mean something—to them and to you. Amazing work." My heart swelled—with pride, but also with a deeper knowing that what he said was true. This journey has filled a need I didn't know I had. It has brought light to those not always seen, filled my heart and studio with joy, and given me purpose in my craft.

That glimpse into his perspective was a gift from God—a confirmation of what I already knew deep down. I shouldn't have needed a worldly affirmation, because this path has always been led by Him. But in that moment, when my artistry brushed against the world's version of success, I felt the cracks of doubt fill in. I knew again, with absolute certainty, that this is where I belong—where God wants me, and where I want to be. Thank you to the Down syndrome community for opening your hearts and arms to me, and for giving my art form, purpose, and direction—and a whole lot of love.

That art form Cami describes has captured the hearts of so many inside and outside the Down syndrome community. She once came to my house for a studio session with five families touched by Down syndrome. I watched her come alive interacting with her subjects, and I had the privilege of seeing the final product of that photo shoot. While I'm sure her photography was superb before launching into the disability community, there is an unmistakable, nuanced quality to the images she produces. It almost feels like the extraordinary joy is leaping out to grab you. She is clearly looking through a different lens than most.

While we are on the subject of lenses, check out what David and Jackson Hughens, a father-son, filmmaking duo have to say about this subject.

Open Eyes, Open Hearts

By Jackson Hughens, Father-son Filmmaking Duo and allies to the Down syndrome community

"I knew you since you were tiny" is what my friend Jay would say when I ask him about our first time meeting each other. He's not wrong either. I was a small, boyish 15-year-old when we met. And though I looked like the child, he was far more in touch with the healthy childlike worldview that I'd already lost in my time as a teenager. My perspective on life, people and the world had shrunk to a tiny spec, and Jay split it wide open that fateful meeting on my spring break trip to Atlanta.

When my dad and I rolled up to stay with our family-friend, I had no clue Jay was waiting on the other side of the door. I had no idea they'd adopted a 21-year-old man with Down syndrome. I had no way of knowing I'd be welcomed with a warm hug, an invitation to color Disney princesses and offered a spa level pedicure. Jay invited me right into his space and offered me the best of what he had. As I watched my dad lean in and become Jay's new best friend, I struggled to compute this type of welcome.

My peers did not value inclusion. In fact it was more about desperately seeking validation from others so that you wouldn't be excluded. It didn't help that the special education students were tucked away in separate buildings and at lunchtime seated in the corner of the cafeteria. The worldview was clear to me; your worth comes from what you can achieve and if you're unable to achieve or maintain appearances you will not have a place in this world. Among my "typical" peers we found things to desperately build our worth upon whether academics, sports, or in my case filmmaking. Atlanta was quickly becoming the Hollywood of the South and I wanted to move there after high school to work for Cartoon Network. So we visited over spring break to dream of what a future in Georgia may look like and that's when Jay began to open up my heart.

I wish I could say that first meeting opened up my limited view, but it would take the next few years of my family friend's holiday gatherings as I finished up school and moved to Atlanta. I began looking forward to my coloring time with Jay. It was a safe haven from awkward conversations of me trying to convince older adults that I had my career all figured out. Jay accepted me for who I was as a person and it wasn't until a couple years of living in the same city that he realized I was in the business of making movies.

My dad and I were coloring with Jay the Thanksgiving after the pandemic when he told us "My grandma always told me to shine my light. You need to put me in a movie." My dad looked up at Jay, "What would the movie be about?" Jay's eyes twinkled "When you wake up tomorrow, think about me and write." Two weeks later my dad had a finished screenplay for a fictional story inspired by Jay's personality and heart. That same heart that took my limited spec of a worldview and opened it wide. When I read the script I knew this was exactly the movie the world needs to see. If there's some 15-year-old out there who's not fortunate enough to meet Jay by fate like I did, then they could at least meet him through the silver screen.

After a few years of pitching and promoting "Made With Love," we still haven't raised the money to produce the film. I understand the process of green-lighting a film takes years but regardless of what happens going forward, I will be grateful for how I've grown to know Jay as my best friend, creative collaborator, and introduction into the Down syndrome community where I've been so fortunate to meet so many brilliant people shining bright. Jay opened up my world and for that I am forever grateful.

Jackson's father, David, the other half of their filmmaking crew, had his own perspective to share about connecting with Jay.

Fully Human

By David Hughens, Father-son Filmmaking Duo and allies to the Down syndrome community

I took up Jay's challenge and wrote a screenplay called "Made With Love" that has won more than 40 awards in film festivals around the world. We enjoyed our time with Jay and then began to immerse ourselves in the Down syndrome community. We made promotional videos for Jay's movie project, the comments on social media posts began to grow and catch our attention. We noticed that there were many touching stories out there about people with Down syndrome. That's when the idea hit us. While we are trying to raise the money to tell Jay's story, let's travel around and tell all these other amazing stories.

That's when "Stories Made With Love" was born, a short form documentary series, and we hit the road. We made a co-branding deal with a nonprofit called RODS Heroes and we have filmed close to 30 videos that have amassed over 75 million views. We didn't have any relatives with Down syndrome, nor did we have much of a connection to the Down syndrome community at all before this endeavor. But since meeting Jay and so many people in the Down syndrome community throughout our travels, we've learned that each and every person is different and unique, full of love and joy, grit and determination, compassion and empathy. They have shown us what it means to be human and fully engaged with those around us.

If someone thanks us for what we are doing, we often say that we are blessed and grateful to get to meet and film these beautiful souls. We see worth and value where maybe we were a little blind before. We see the need for inclusion and seek to include where maybe we avoided before. We see the need for advocacy where maybe we were too silent before. We know that we have a greater capacity for love after spending time with our friends with Down syndrome.

Seventy-five million viewers have gotten a glimpse of the magic. . .the divinity of Down syndrome. . .through the work they have created, alongside RODS Heroes. Seventy-five million eyes have tasted and seen that Down syndrome is not something to fear. And while they have worked tirelessly, filming families all over the globe, the fabric of their hearts continues to grow and change as they meet each unique individual with Down syndrome. That's the power of connection. That's the power of exposure. That's the power of inclusion.

In October, for Down syndrome awareness month, I went to Jed's classroom to share with the students about Down syndrome. I read a book written by Brady Murray, Founder of RODS Heroes, called "Cooper is Super and So are You" which is all about finding the superpowers in each of us. It's about discovering, uncovering and celebrating the unique abilities within each and every person.

I noticed that the children in Jed's class readily and eagerly pointed out what made Jed super. I'm not sure that I, at their age, would have been able to recognize the gift of someone like Jed because I didn't have exposure to anyone with Down syndrome. I marveled at their open hearts and minds and admired their ability to point out what was super within themselves, as well. Because when we have the ability to recognize the innate beauty and value in EVERY person, it's a whole lot easier to find it within ourselves.

What if every single person on this planet had a chance to get to know someone with Down syndrome? Not just a one-time introduction but a true and real relationship?! How would that change the way the world sees Down syndrome? I would venture to say that this personal connection would change everything. Because to know someone with Down syndrome is to love someone with Down syndrome.

A Little Extra

So much of this experience can be difficult to navigate. Especially in the beginning. Fear of saying the "Wrong" thing can lead to not saying or doing anything at all. It is my sincere hope that this book helps equip some who feel this way. Taking the time to educate yourself about the community and, better yet, getting to know someone with Down syndrome can alleviate the fear that is often prevalent. Ask questions, get curious, and SHOW UP for your loved one who is experiencing this unexpected road. It's not about being right all the time or having all (or any) of the answers. It's simply about entering a new landscape with open palms and a willing heart.

CHAPTER 14

A Word from Self-Advocates

"We are so much more than our disabilities, even if history depicts us wrongly. What makes us who we are is what we choose to be now, and how we give back to the world, for better or worse, is a determinant of who we are as people. I believe in a world where everyone gets along and celebrates our differences as one community."

—Dashiell Meyer, Self-advocate with Down syndrome

I have a confession to make, and I hope one or two of you can relate. As a fierce advocate for my five-year-old son, I can sometimes speak out without thinking things through. I'm a passionate, often impulsive, person, and the urge to voice my opinion before listening and learning to self-advocates can be strong. The reality is, there are adults with Down syndrome who have much to say about the life they are leading. We just need to be willing to have ears to listen.

So listen we shall . . .

This chapter is filled with the words of self-advocates in their teens and twenties, starting with Audrey and Jeremy who are the dynamic duo behind The Audrey and Jeremy Show—a podcast where they sit down with "World Changers" who are using their voices and talents to make the world a better place. Lifelong friends turned couple, Audrey and Jeremy bring heart, humor, and honesty to every conversation. Together, they're breaking stereotypes, celebrating inclusion, and inspiring others to lead with kindness and confidence.

Beyond the podcast, they, along with their best friend, Mason, co-founded Down Syndrome Rocks, a nonprofit dedicated to creating meaningful employment and promoting self-advocacy for individuals with Down syndrome. Audrey is an actor, model, public speaker, and fierce self-advocate studying drama and communications in college, with a passion for storytelling and connection. Jeremy is a SAG Actor, public speaker, self-advocate, mentor, and West Coast Ambassador for A Walk on Water, inspiring others through movement, mentorship, and community.

Whether they're behind the mic, on stage, or in the community, Audrey and Jeremy are leading with heart—amplifying voices, celebrating abilities, and proving that with inclusion and opportunity, everyone can shine. Since they are an incredible podcasting team, it only seemed appropriate to have them share in an interview format! Before they began, Audrey and Jeremy wanted to mutually agree on the definition of the words, "Advocate" and "Self Advocate." So that's how it began . . .

- **"Advocate"**—a person who communicates support for a cause or need
- A **Self Advocate** is a person who can communicate what they want or need.

Audrey and Jeremy agreed they are both of those things.

What qualities help you to be an Advocate?
Audrey: Confidence, willingness to help the community and to make a difference.
Jeremy: Good eye contact!
Audrey: Good conversationalist.

In raising you, what did your parents do that helped you to have confidence?
Audrey: I think growing up, it was easier for my parents when I was a baby. I was super cute. Later, it was challenging for them to get me to do stuff like make my bed and stuff.

They helped me by making me take responsibility for my actions and things that I did. . . like stabbing my brother's iPad with a sharpie. I regretted doing that.
Jeremy: The way they saw me in the community, when I clicked with A Walk on Water for example. My parents saw the confidence in me to be surfing on my own—independently!

Growing up, what helped you realize you wanted to make a difference in your community?
Audrey: I love to make a difference in my community, like inclusion for people with disabilities like me. I was involved in all different activities. Having a great life can start with support staff and getting active. What they need. Support staff for each person with a disability is important because everybody's unique in their different ways."
Jeremy: I always wanted to do that and since I was born until now 25 years old telling you this now that this community is going to have a huge difference!

Growing up you participated in both inclusive activities AND specialty activities (and education). What are the benefits of each?
Jeremy: Getting new friends is what is mostly important in all activities. In Hoop Stars (specialty) I got to learn who I was. Then in inclusion, I knew who I was.
Audrey: Building friendships and relationships can happen at all the activities. I think specialty programs are important for parents so that they feel a sense of belonging. And get more information.

What made you decide on Producing a Podcast?
Audrey: We love to talk to people, so our families' agreed that this would expand our vocabulary, get invited to different things and we have!
Jeremy: It is a lot of fun to talk to people about their stories! And their jobs for our community!
Audrey: Jobs that help to make good change in our community!

Audrey and Jeremy continue to have groundbreaking, important conversations through their podcast and other forms of media. They are doing incredibly valuable and necessary advocacy work in the Down syndrome community and beyond.

They aren't the only ones, either!

Sofia Sanchez is a Ukrainian American teenage actress, model, advocate, and influencer known for her viral video "Down Syndrome Is Not Scary." She had her acting debut in the TV series Switched at Birth and has also appeared in the films For Paloma and later this year in The Hunger Games: The Ballad of Songbirds and Snakes. She's done print ads and commercials for legacy retail brands like Old Navy and Target and made her first voice-over appearance in a popular Nickelodeon cartoon in 2024. Additionally, her adoption story has inspired several picture books with Scholastic, including *You Are Enough and You Are Love* and her third book *You Are Brave*, which came out in 2024. Her TedTalk inspired many, and she is always ready to talk about her personal, lived experience with anyone willing to listen. Here's what she has to say about living a life with an extra chromosome.

> "Down syndrome is one part of who I am but I am not scared that I have disability in me because some kids have Down syndrome and some kids don't have Down syndrome. But it's ok. Everyone can be different and they can all be loved. Everyone can be special in a different way. I am brave because I did some hard things in my life. I did a big TEDx Talk speech and I was nervous but I didn't let fear hold me back. I've been zip lining in Mexico City and I was scared but I said, 'OK, I got this, I can do this!' And I did it. I was brave. Some kids are sometimes sad when they don't have parents, that they want so badly. They just need parents to come and love them and give them a loving family. When I was an orphan in Ukraine, I wanted a mom, I wanted a dad, I wanted pets, I wanted brothers, I wanted school, I wanted friends, I wanted neighbors. And guess what? THEY CAME and helped me! Fear made me an orphan but bravery gave me a family. There is power in being brave. That's why my family chose me and I chose them right back! And that's how we love each other as a family. My mom and dad went to this orphanage that I was born in. Kids can follow their own dreams in their hearts to make their lives a beautiful place!"[1]

Sofia is such a beautiful representation of a young lady in the Down syndrome community, sharing her gifts generously with the world. There are many talented artists with Down syndrome throughout the world, but we have to have our eyes fully open to see that. In an earlier chapter, I described my experience watching a high schooler with Down syndrome in a musical, just the day before my diagnosis. Sadly, she was my FIRST exposure to someone with Down syndrome onstage. But she most definitely wouldn't be the last.

A couple of years into Jed's life, I saw a video of a young girl with Down syndrome singing the Star Spangled Banner for a Down syndrome buddy walk and was blown away by this girl's voice. I searched high and low for more information on this girl and discovered her name was Mia.

Mia Rodriguez is a 16-year-old powerhouse performer, passionate self-advocate, and rising voice in the world of music, disability representation, and inclusion. With her unique blend of vocal talent and fearless authenticity, Mia is capturing both national and international attention—on stage, on screen, and in the advocacy world. Mia's journey into self-advocacy began in elementary school, when she recorded short videos to express her thoughts and share her voice during IEP meetings. In middle school, she began leading her own IEPs and made it her mission to help others understand the power of voice and self-determination. Now in her sophomore year of high school, Mia is fully included and continues advocating for herself as part of a peer mentoring program. Off-stage, Mia has spoken at statewide conferences and lobbied in Washington, DC, using her story to promote visibility, inclusion, and acceptance for all people with disabilities. Her mission is rooted in joy, voice, and visibility—because she believes everyone deserves to be seen, heard, and included. She dreams of a future where she can combine her passions for music and fashion while continuing to break down barriers—one song at a time. Mia lives in Pennsylvania with her parents and two younger siblings and continues to inspire others by being unapologetically herself—on and off stage. Here's what she has to say about living life with Down syndrome.

A Star Is Born!

By Mia Rodriguez, Self-advocate

I love my life! I am a teenager with Down syndrome, and advocating is a big part of who I am because my future belongs to me. When I speak up in my IEP meetings or any other meeting, or when I share my singing on stage or stories online, people get to see the real me. I want them to hear my own voice, my dreams, and my goals, and not just what others imagine for me.

Sometimes that means telling my teachers what makes me feel overwhelmed, or reminding adults to treat me my age. Other times it's standing on a stage, singing and performing with passion so the world knows we all have something important to give. Advocacy is asking for help when I need it, but it's more than that. It's about showing people that I have something to say, something to share, and a future full of possibility and that matters. And along the way, I know I have so much to learn from people around me, but I also believe people learn from me too. Isn't that a beautiful thing?

Looking to my future, I know I will keep using my voice to break stereotypes and open doors; not only for myself, but for others like me. Like many teenagers, I have big dreams too. I want to record my own songs, be on Broadway one day, and maybe even combine music and fashion to create shows where everyone feels welcome. I know I'll need support along the way, and that's okay, because everyone does. What matters most is that people believe in me and in all young people with disabilities.

I want new parents to know that Down syndrome is not something to fear. Our lives are meant to be celebrated, simply for who we are, for the joy and connection we bring. And when given the chance, we can grow, learn, love, and live meaningful lives, just like anyone else.

Mia is absolutely stepping into her calling and reaching people like me who had little to no exposure to those living with Trisomy 21.

Similarly, Matthew Schwab has stepped boldly into his calling and a few words of encouragement to share to those who may be new to the journey

Matthew Speaks to *You*

By Matthew Schwab, Self-advocate

So, you're having a baby with Down syndrome? Let me tell you a little about me and my life. I also have Down syndrome! I am Matthew Schwab and I am a 28-year-old North Carolina native. I'm an advocate, actor, volunteer, board member, and public speaker. I love my life.

I am an athlete with the Special Olympics, I live in a condo with my gorgeous fiancé, I ballroom dance, I am a restaurant host, a brother, and a role model. I want to continue living my best life.

To me, Down syndrome is something special and we should celebrate all accomplishments together as human beings. I would not trade my extra chromosome for anything. It has made me who I am.

As an adult who has Down syndrome, I have a unique perspective, and I think hearing my story may give hope to you. It shows everyone . . . community members, teachers, employers, and even family members . . . what is possible. Don't be scared. Embrace your baby and be patient. Great things are ahead.

We heard from Amy Julia Becker about her experience with her daughter Penny in the chapter "Once the Bus Stops Coming." Now it's time to hear from Penny, herself, about her life! She is a second year student in Post University's UPP Program. She loves reading, writing, dance, The Summer I Turned Pretty, and Taylor Swift. She lives with her parents and her younger brother and sister in Watertown, Connecticut.

Finding Her Way Through Higher Education

By Penny Becker, Self-advocate

My name is Penny Becker, and I am 19 years old with Down syndrome. I like to read and write, and I try to improve my writing every day. In 2024, I graduated from Shepaug Valley High School. In high school, I enjoyed being a part of a senior project class, watching boys play soccer and basketball, and all the school dances, but I didn't always feel included. The thing that I miss most about high school is cheerleading.

We got introduced to Post University, which is in Waterbury, Connecticut. I have been there for two years now. The program I am in is a transition program for all ages and disabilities. Post is a commuter college, so I still live at home. The program lets you audit classes and gives you a worksite where you go two days a week with different groups of people.

At first, college was tough. One example is making new friends. Another example is not having everything planned out for the afternoons. The social life on a college campus is still challenging for me. I am now in my second year of college, and things are going pretty well. I am taking an English: Power of Words class, which focuses on writing. I feel a tighter bond in my friendships this year than last year. I've learned two things over the two years I have been in college. Sometimes change is a good thing, and friendships are the most important thing.

It's so impactful to hear stories like Penny's because it wasn't long ago that many people didn't think it was possible for individuals to walk or talk, let alone go to college. Yet Penny and many of her peers are exploring how they want to live and lead their lives. Peers like Dashiell Meier an animator, self-advocate, storyteller, filmmaker, college student, and athlete. Here's more about him!

The Sky Is the Limit

By Dashiell Meier, Self-advocate

I have Trisomy 21/Down syndrome! I have been doing what I can to help my community. I am a self-advocate for people with disabilities, and I work with disability groups like Special Olympics and the National Down Syndrome Society. I spoke at the United Nations about health equity for people with Down syndrome. I have made it my personal mission to ensure that everyone, like me and others, looks past the prejudice about us to find meaning and self-pride. I am proud to have Trisomy 21!

That is why I am majoring in film and media, as an extension of my advocacy to show the world that the things that make us different only make us stronger than ever. I am currently attending Foothill College in Los Altos, where I am taking film classes to enhance my filmmaking skills. Some of my projects include Day 21, an award-winning short thriller I made for the Easterseals Disability Film Challenge about a post-apocalyptic world where there are only people with Down syndrome left. I also made an award-winning documentary short all by myself about what I want people to know about Down syndrome called This Is Me. I am working on my first documentary feature, which explores the history of Down syndrome, and my first 3D animated short, titled 321.

I love my community and family, and everything I have accomplished in my life so far is a result of their support and help, which fills me with great gratitude. But most of all, I want everyone who reads this book to look back on what they have accomplished so far and tell the people who have been by their side their whole life just how much their support will live on for years to come.

For families just receiving a Down syndrome diagnosis, I want to say to you all that having children with Down syndrome or any disability is a blessing to have because we have so much to offer this world. Let us experience life, including

(*continued*)

its mistakes. We all want the same treatment as everyone else, like being included in schools, and we need our parents' support. One way to do so is to understand that people with disabilities are just as human as everyone else.

I encourage all parents to work together to create a better world for all groups of people. You can start by seeing your child with disabilities in a new light and believe they can accomplish their dreams.

A Little Extra

We can listen to what society says about disability, or we can listen to disability advocates themselves. We can hear THEM when they share about the ups and downs of their lived experience. Each one of these self-advocates have rich, personal, individualized life experiences to share about as a person with Down syndrome. And they can and should be the mouthpiece to speak about what it's like navigating their own path. Let's listen. Let's take the time to learn what they want for their lives.

My five-year-old, Jed, has a mantra that he shouts from the rooftops whenever he tries something he couldn't do before and succeeds. ***"I DID IT!"*** A self-advocate in the making!

CHAPTER 15

The Road to Adoption

"Not of my flesh, nor of my bone, but still miraculously my own. Never forget for a single minute, you didn't grow under my heart, but in it."

—Fleur Conkling Heyliger

People actually adopt children with Down syndrome?

I'll never forget reading that question in the comment sections of a reel I'd created after visiting Armenia with RODS Heroes. We had gone to an orphanage, and I had fallen in love with so many beautiful children like my Jed. I wanted to bring them all home and shower them with love. I also know from personal experience that people with Down syndrome have so much love and affection to give and share. It was heartbreaking seeing them in an environment where they might not be able to give and receive that kind of affection. Not because the staff wasn't wonderful—they were. But because there were so many children there and only so many workers to care for their needs.

In my eagerness to share as much as I could about these children with Down syndrome who did not have homes, I'd created a reel of videos and pictures of my time in Armenia. Most of the response was overwhelmingly good and positive. Many people inquired on how *they* might adopt, and I gladly passed along some information to the adoption agency with which we traveled. However, the comment section was also filled with incredulous individuals who could not grasp *why* anyone would choose to adopt a child with Down syndrome. It simultaneously broke my heart and made me angry. But when I stepped back and surveyed the situation, I realized:

They just don't know.

As we've covered in multiple sections of this book, people don't know or understand what they have not yet come to know or understand. I may have asked that same question before I gave birth to Jed. Exposure and inclusion is everything in breaking down that invisible wall dividing fear and embrace.

The families in this chapter are gracious enough to share their personal stories of acceptance into this new life.

Scariest and Best Yes

By Heather Avis, Mother, Advocate, Speaker, NY Times Best Selling Author

I was sitting on a springy bed in a two-star motel at the base of the Transylvania Mountains near Cluj-Napoca, Romania, when I opened an email that changed my life.

But let me back up.

Two years earlier, after years of infertility, my husband and I had begun the journey of adoption. We dreamed of a healthy infant, so when we filled out the forms, we carefully checked "no" in every box that suggested otherwise. A year later, we became an official waiting family.

Fast forward one year. My husband and I were leading a church team on a trip to Romania, spending two weeks hosting youth camps. The night before we left, I emailed our social worker: "While I'm not expecting anything to happen, I just wanted to let you know we'll be out of the country from July 23–Aug. 7. We'll check email occasionally if you need to reach us."

The next day, we boarded a plane. At the end of the trip, we checked into a tiny mountain motel. I opened my laptop to catch up on email, and there it was—a reply from our social worker:

> "Your profile has been shown once. Things are slow. We've recently had a few babies with Down syndrome placed with us, and finding homes for them has been a little more difficult."

I read those words, and my heart stopped. I didn't want a baby with Down syndrome. That was never the plan. Our social worker wasn't suggesting this baby for us—just giving an update. But suddenly I couldn't un-know what I now knew:

- A baby.
- A baby with Down syndrome.
- A baby with Down syndrome in need of a family.

I told my husband. We looked at each other, and we both knew: we couldn't ignore this.

For the rest of the trip, we prayed and we talked. I felt torn in two. I did not want to raise a child with Down syndrome, and I did not want to say no. On our last night, overlooking the Aegean Sea, we made a pros and cons list.

Pro: Baby

Con: Down syndrome

That was it. That was all we knew.

When we got home, we called our social worker and said we wanted to learn more. And a few months later, we said yes to a baby girl born with Down syndrome.

Her name is Macyn Hope. She came home on October 29, 2008—my scariest and best "yes."

I will never forget that first night. I carried her into the nursery I had so carefully prepared. She fell asleep as I put her in pink pajamas with little hearts. I sat down in the old green chair in the corner, gazed at her tiny face, and whispered, "Huh. I can't seem to remember what I was so afraid of."

(*continued*)

Seventeen years have passed since that night. Not a single day has gone by when I haven't thanked God for leading us to each other.

I think back often to that pros and cons list. We placed Down syndrome in the con column. But it took less than 24 hours as Macyn's mother for me to see the truth:

Down syndrome was never the con. It has always been the gift. To know and love a person with Down syndrome makes me the luckiest person I know.

So many times in life, we think the path will look a certain way until we come to a major fork in the road. There have been many forks encountered on my journey, and I am well aware of how difficult it can be to take that *one* step into the unknown. But once you've walked into that Secret Garden of love and opened your eyes to the beauty of Down syndrome, it's difficult to divert your eyes again. Chantelle experienced this with her daughters, Selah and Lilly.

From Foster Care to Adoption

By Chantelle McMullin, Adoptive and Biological Mom in the Down syndrome community

In the beginning it was just my husband, our three-year-old son Ethan, and me. Life felt steady and full, and while we were already fostering, we decided it was the right time to add one more biological child to our family. That pregnancy felt so beautiful and perfect. I became pregnant easily, and when we found out it was a girl I was ecstatic. It felt like one more piece falling into place for our picture-perfect family. Everything seemed certain, like we were stepping into the happiest chapter yet.

At 26 weeks, everything changed. We learned that our daughter Selah would be born with Down syndrome. It felt like the world I had so carefully pictured for our family had been turned upside down. I worried about what our life would look like. Would we still be able to foster, to travel, to live the life we had imagined? Selah came into our lives and showed us that she was everything we never knew we needed. She opened our eyes to how beautiful life with Down syndrome could be. We often laugh now and say that one wasn't enough.

That truth came alive when Lilly entered our home through foster care. Only a week before, we had gone through a very emotional and physically exhausting placement disruption. I was at one of my lowest points, certain that I did not want to foster again, and we even considered closing our home. In the end, we decided to take a break instead. A week later, during that break, my placement manager called. She said, "I know you're not open to more placements right now, but this case fell in our lap and your name came up over and over in the meeting. There's a little baby in the NICU who has been abandoned for almost four months. She has Down syndrome, and she needs a foster home that could possibly adopt her."

At the time, we actually felt called to adopt a child with Down syndrome and were beginning the process of possibly adopting from Ukraine. We had no idea that adoption through foster care was even a possibility since reunification is always the first goal. It felt like a huge decision. At first we hesitated—we had never taken in a baby or a child with significant medical needs. But the team gently persuaded us, assuring us she might be similar to our other child with Down syndrome. Of course, we learned very quickly that Lilly was completely unique, as every child is.

Lilly had survived so much in her short life. She was born at just one pound, without a heartbeat and not breathing. She had suffered two grade four brain bleeds after a traumatic birth,

(*continued*)

which led to her later diagnosis of cerebral palsy. She came to us at nearly four months old, weighing just seven pounds, dependent on oxygen at night and with a G-tube.

Bringing her home was the beginning of a new chapter. It took three long years of navigating the system before her adoption was finalized. It was both beautiful and heartbreaking: beautiful because she finally had permanency with us, heartbreaking because it marked the finality of her biological family's choices. In the end, reunification was simply not an option, and permanency was the safest and best path for her.

Today Lilly is thriving. She is resilient, joyful, and strong. Looking back, I am so glad we did not close our home after that hard season. Saying yes to Lilly changed our family forever. Now our family feels complete. The fear I once carried, the belief that life as we knew it was over, has given way to the truth that this life is the greatest gift. We fell in love not only with our daughters, but with Down syndrome itself. The stigma we once carried, the assumption that we could never foster children with special needs, was rooted in ignorance and ableism. What we learned is that we are not "special" parents. We are just parents. Selah and Lilly have transformed our hearts, our family, and our future. They prove every day that dreams can take unexpected shapes and still turn out more beautiful than anything we could have planned.

The greatest gift we can give to ourselves and to those we love most is to open our door to disability. It is a path that can be wrought with challenges and twists and turns. But it is also a transformative, radically life-altering experience to open your arms to a new way of life. Those of us in the Down syndrome community come to a place of recognition about that and it stops being a question of *Why would someone adopt a child with Down syndrome* and it starts becoming a question of *Why doesn't everyone adopt a child with Down syndrome!*

Two Children with Down Syndrome. One Big Heart

By Jennifer Sanchez, Advocate, Mom in the Down syndrome community

I have the great honor of being a parent of two children with Down syndrome. I have a biological son with Down syndrome named Joaquin and we adopted Sofia from Ukraine. Joaquin initially opened our eyes to this beautiful world of disability and opened our eyes to the need for orphans with Down syndrome. What I was experiencing with Joaquin was very special. There are challenges and there are worries. But the love that I was feeling and the connection I had with him was so special that I just couldn't imagine babies not having that with a family.

I decided I would donate to an organization that had babies with disabilities up for adoption. About a week later I got an envelope from them and in it was an ornament with a picture of Sofia on it. We hung it on our Christmas tree and something instantly happened in me. There I was trying to help this baby find a family so that she could live a beautiful life. But I thought, "Why aren't we the ones doing that? Why not us?" So, we got on a plane to Ukraine. We brought Sofia home, and Joaquin and Sofia were instantly connected. It was beautiful but it was scary because I thought, "Is she ever going to feel like my biological children?" But I woke up one day and I couldn't imagine my life without her. The bond and connection took time but definitely happened. The light and the joy that I experienced with my son was there with Sofia but in her own unique and beautiful way.

There's an urgency for me to share because I want a world that values them as much as I do. Every human wants to feel accepted for who they are and that's what I hope to build for them. This is a beautiful life that we never expected to have, and I would encourage parents on this path to be open to what happens and look at the beauty that can come from that. Your whole life plan may be something you never dreamed of but when you trust, open your heart, and offer love and support to those in great need like an orphan, it's so rewarding. Every baby deserves the chance to shine whatever light they have, just like Joaquin and Sofia.

Many in the Down syndrome community use the word *magic* to describe the experience of crossing into the tucked away garden they hadn't explored before. Whether you are contemplating adopting a child with Down syndrome, have just adopted, or you did so long ago, there is no question that magic will come your way. It can also be described as simply . . . divine.

As a friend or family member trying to support a loved one going along on this journey, it's so important to read the real words of others who have walked this path.

Inspired by Down Syndrome to Adopt

By Brady Murray, Founder of RODS Heroes, Speaker, Author and Dad in the Down syndrome community

Our son Nash was given a birth diagnosis of Down syndrome. Before we knew this information, I had been filled with anticipation to meet him and fulfill aspirations of what I thought life would look like with my firstborn son. I had pictured all of the father-son activities we'd be doing together. The camping, fishing, hunting and the baseball games that we'd be attending. I pictured him playing baseball and I would be coaching! So, when my wife and I heard about his Down syndrome diagnosis within minutes of Nash being born, it seemed like that version of what I envisioned was completely gone, and I was gripped with fear. I'm an ultra planner, charting out family vacations three, four years in advance to make sure the scheduling works and we get the right reservation. And so for me, Mr. Planner, I charted exactly what our life was going to look like.

With the birth of Nash, it initially seemed like all of that was gone. It took me a number of months, if not years, to finally be able to come to like a place of acceptance with Nash and his diagnosis. I never felt a feeling of resentment or any type of negativity toward him specifically, but I definitely felt the weight of a very different life than what I had planned. I wondered what this would mean for my wife and me after our retirement and my thoughts were very self-focused. Through raising Nash, however, I learned that people who have Down Syndrome have a very special way of helping us get outside of ourselves, which is truly a unique superpower.

In those early days, I never could have envisioned adopting another child with Down syndrome. Of the 8 billion people in the world, there are maybe a million that truly understand the superpower of Down syndrome and would accept, embrace, and celebrate a diagnosis of Down syndrome. Ninety-nine percent of the world population, if given the choice to have a child with Down syndrome or to have a typical child, would choose to have a typical child. But once your life has been touched by Down syndrome, there is no going back. There is no un-feeling the magic. So it makes sense that some families like mine, who have a biological child with Down syndrome, would choose to adopt another one. You're already on the path and experiencing the highs and lows of the journey.

But what's truly incredible to witness, as I've spent years as a dad in the Down syndrome community, are the many families we've helped adopt who don't already have a child with Down syndrome. To choose to enter into the journey of Down syndrome is a beautiful and remarkable thing.

When Nash was four years old, my family and I started getting involved in the Down syndrome community. From an advocating standpoint, this was the time we learned about the many thousands of children with Down syndrome throughout the world that were (and are) in need of adoption. We decided to do something about it through a Racing Iron Man's forum, we created a foundation forum, and we helped inspire many families to adopt a child with Down syndrome. During this time, people would often ask me, "Brady, when are you guys going to adopt a child with Down syndrome?"

I responded by saying, "We already have a child with Down syndrome." My wife Andrea and I HAD talked about adoption our whole marriage and even when we were dating. But we had never once talked about adopting a child with Down syndrome. Andrea was the one that introduced the concept to me

(*continued*)

and the notion of it took me right back to many of the feelings and emotions in the delivery room with Nash. The fear, and the unknown.

Over time, my wife and I processed through that and we began pondering adoption. But we did what you do in those important times of your life when you make important, life-changing, generational decisions and we made it a matter of prayer and pondering. In my heart, I knew it was something that we were supposed to do and so we went for it, despite my fears and some of those reluctances that I had.

Fast forward to now and it's been nine years since we adopted Cooper. I'm so thankful I didn't let fear get in the way. Our lives are so much better with Cooper in our family. And through this experience of raising awareness for adoption, we began what would become RODS Heroes.

What started with just a group of neighborhood guys doing some racing, some triathlons, and some Iron Man triathlons to help children with Down Syndrome find their forever home, evolved into a full-fledged foundation that is inspiring hundreds of families to be able to adopt a child with Down syndrome. Instead of focusing on racing, we're allocating time to be able to do the work of RODS Heroes where our mission has evolved from not only inspiring families to answer the call to adopt, but broadly seeking to uncover the superpowers of Down syndrome. Through storytelling and connecting with the community.

For those who have adoption in their hearts but are feeling unsure or fearful, I would say that those feelings are very normal and good. Those moments of pause are there as a protection to help you take this decision seriously. This is not a scenario of just helping a kid out for a short period of time. This is a life-altering, generational impact decision, and so it's one that you want to measure twice before ultimately making a decision to move forward.

But if you are feeling a nudge, those feelings are often there for a reason. Some may call it intuition or a gut feeling, or others like me consider it a nudge from God. When we follow that intuition, that spirit, and those feelings, we can take courage that in every situation, it will all work out for the better. It doesn't mean that it's going to be sunshine and rainbows all the time. As my daughter pointed out a few weeks ago, in her 19-year-old wisdom, "Just because it's hard doesn't mean that it's not right."

If you adopt a child with Down syndrome, you will experience hardship. You will get out of your comfort zone. You will be forced to face insecurities and weaknesses. You will experience challenges and roadblocks that you might not have ever faced if you didn't choose to go down this path. But similar to everything that's worth doing in life, those experiences will bring growth and have a meaningful impact for years to come. Your children and children's children are going to benefit from having the superpower of Down syndrome in their lives.

To all my fellow dads on this Down syndrome journey, it is natural and good to want to be the protector of the family and the one who wants to carry the family along in the hard times. What I have found, in relation to adoption and with a Down syndrome diagnosis, is that there are opportunities to let down our guard. Sometimes we have to remove our armor and allow ourselves to be vulnerable. To ask for and receive help.

When I spoke at a DSDN Rockin' Dad's Retreat this summer, it was very clear that each of us felt many of the same insecurities that come with walking the road of raising a loved one with a disability. It was a healing and therapeutic experience to connect with those dads—my community. My admonition and encouragement to any dads that are on this journey, whether you have a child who you've adopted or a child that you know is your biological child, is to seek to surround yourself with other dads who are on the same journey, and allow yourself to be vulnerable. In the end, you'll be a lot stronger for it.

A Little Extra

If you are considering adopting a child with Down syndrome, there are many organizations to explore that involve adoption to varying degrees. The National Down Syndrome Adoption Network (NDSAN).

Is a free domestic adoption program and registry. Families can create a profile to be matched with children, and the network provides information and support to both birth and adoptive families. RODS Heroes, mentioned above, advocates for orphans all throughout the globe and shines a light on their individuals with Down syndrome through storytelling. There are many children with Down syndrome waiting in the foster care system. Adopting from foster care often has little to no fee and may include a monthly subsidy to help with the child's care until they reach adulthood.

When considering adoption, it's important to be aware of potential medical needs that some children with Down syndrome have, such as heart issues or sleep apnea. It's also noteworthy that raising a child with Down syndrome is a lifelong commitment. Some adults with Down syndrome live independently, while others require more extensive support.

CHAPTER 16

Organizations for Your Tool Belt

> *"What is home? My favorite definition is "a safe place," a place where one is free from attack, a place where one experiences secure relationships and affirmation. It's a place where people share and understand each other. Its relationships are nurturing. The people in it do not need to be perfect; instead, they need to be honest, loving, supportive, recognizing a common humanity that makes all of us vulnerable."*
>
> —Gladys Hunt

In this chapter, you'll learn about several organizations that have been an integral part of my journey (you can find the URLs of each organization in the "Resource List" at the end of the book). The people who devote their lives to this work don't just give you a paper of statistics and call it a day. The people behind these organizations are passionate about spreading awareness, encouragement, joy, and resources. When I first scrolled through a list of these organizations after a frantic google search, I didn't have the slightest idea about what they were about or what services they provided. I would skim websites and testimonials in search of the tiniest tidbit of encouragement and direction. It was absolutely exhausting.

The most tiring part of all of it was the technical jargon I didn't yet understand and the prescriptive feel of everything I was reading. I *wanted* people. I *needed* people. In keeping with that, I decided to reach out to specific people within some of these organizations so you could hear the heart behind the mission and the stories behind the work. It made all the difference for me and connected the dots of so many unending and directionless lines on a page.

Down Syndrome Diagnosis Network (DSDN)

The mission of the Down Syndrome Diagnosis Network is to connect, support, and provide accurate information to parents—and the medical professionals who serve them—from the time of diagnosis through age three while fostering the opportunity for lifelong connections. Their vision is that every Down syndrome diagnosis will be delivered in an unbiased, factual, and supportive way every time and that families can quickly find meaningful connections.

About DSDN

By Jen Jacob, Founder of the DSDN

As an experienced mom of three, I expected to feel confident when welcoming our youngest son. But after learning he would likely have Down syndrome, I suddenly felt like a brand-new parent again. There was so much to learn, and I was overwhelmed as I began processing the diagnosis. I turned to books, websites, and online groups, searching for information and support.

What I found were stories at two extremes—either impossibly perfect or deeply discouraging. I longed for something in the middle. What did real life look like? What could the years beyond the newborn stage hold for our family? I desperately wanted to know whether what I was feeling and experiencing was "normal."

So, I decided to create the space I needed. I invited other new moms in the Down syndrome community to join me, and with that, the first DSDN birth group was born. I quickly realized I wasn't alone—I had found my people.

In the original 2012–2013 Rockin' Mom group, more than 150 moms from around the world shared stories that echoed my own. We had navigated all kinds of diagnosis experiences—the good, the bad, and the heart-wrenching. In sharing openly, we found comfort, strength, and a shared passion for changing the diagnosis experience for the families who would come after us. Through celebrations, tears, and daily life raising children with Down syndrome, we discovered that community could be truly life-changing.

DSDN officially launched in 2014 with a mission to connect, support, and provide accurate information to parents—and the medical professionals who serve them. Our vision is that every Down syndrome diagnosis will be delivered in an unbiased, factual, and compassionate way, and that families can quickly find meaningful support.

A decade later, DSDN supports more than 20,000 parents around the world through online birth groups and topical subgroups, ensuring that all new and expectant parents have access to resources and community. Hundreds of volunteers have served countless hours to provide peer support, host annual mom and dad retreats, and share their diagnosis experiences with medical providers.

New parents often express their gratitude for the support and connection they've found through DSDN. But the truth is—I am equally grateful. I created the first online group because I needed a lifeline during those early days with my son, Owen. That lifeline made all the difference in our family's journey.

Team Iron Will

Team Iron Will celebrates the perseverance of children with Down syndrome and their families. Their mission is to champion the intrinsic value of individuals with Down syndrome as they fulfill God's purpose for their lives by educating families and providers about effective and cutting-edge techniques, procedures, and programs that maximize our children's lived experiences with expert-led sessions offering insights, guidance, and real-life stories.

About Team Iron Will

By Cathy Daub, Co-Founder of Team Iron Will

Will is our 8th child, so bringing him home should have been a piece of cake. But it wasn't. I had a lot of questions. I had a lot of fear. He had a large hole in his heart, and tracheomalacia, which meant that he sounded like he was gasping for air a lot. I remember a particular night where I hadn't slept in at least a week. I'd just sit and stare at this amazing little human to make sure he was breathing. My husband ran out to the store and came back with an Owlet (sock that monitored both Will's heart rate and oxygen level). It restored peace to my weary soul because now if there was a problem, I'd be made aware. It didn't fix the hole in his heart, nor the trouble with his oxygen, but it threw me a lifeline and allowed me to rest so I could better care for him.

We created Team Iron Will so that no parent feels alone on this journey. Part of that is making medical and therapy equipment accessible and affordable. For many families overwhelmed with medical expenses and extra therapies or just being reduced to one income after the baby is born, there isn't always a lot left over for expensive medical equipment. And insurance is not always agreeable to the things our children need.

Families deserve to give their children every chance to thrive. And they deserve to parent out of place of joy rather than fear or constant worry. So, Team Iron Will steps in to help families by providing medical, therapy and adaptive equipment.

Recently a mom said to me "I feel like we had our baby, and they just patted us on the back and said 'good luck' with no real idea of what we needed to help our baby thrive." We felt this too. There are so many incredible resources out there for families in the Down syndrome community. So many unknown but invaluable resources for things like early learning, speech therapy techniques, feeding help, and so much more. But many of those things seem to be hidden and inaccessible. So, we step in there too. We've built relationships with experts in many fields and offer free educational webinars so that parents can learn about the most effective ways to help their children thrive and be given the right tools if they need them.

No one should feel alone on this journey. And at Team Iron Will, we will walk with you, support you, and cheer you on. This journey is beautiful no matter what. But it's sweeter when you know and feel you are not alone.

National Down Syndrome Congress (NDSC)

The National Down Syndrome Congress (NDSC) is a not-for-profit organization dedicated to an improved world for individuals with Down syndrome. Founded in 1973, we are the leading national resource of support and information for anyone touched by or seeking to learn about Down syndrome, from the moment of diagnosis, whether prenatal or at birth, through adulthood.

About NDSC

By Magaly Diaz, the Multicultural Program Coordinator of NDSC

I think I first heard about NDSC when my child was three or four, but back then I was a stay-at-home mom with no means to attend the yearly convention that I knew took place all over the US.

(*continued*)

As a young family, attending one of these was not on our wish list even though we knew it could be valuable to attend.

Now my daughter is 13 years old, I have worked at NDSC for a year and a half and we have attended four conventions. I came to NDSC in March 2024, I saw the job posting early in the year, and I sent in my resume because I knew this is exactly what I was looking for. A role that could make a difference by engaging diverse populations with the organization, not just at convention. Being Bilingual has become my superpower to help people that need information in their language. Before working at NDSC, I didn't know what an international powerhouse it was, bringing people from all over the world to learn more about Down syndrome. In 2022 I attended my first convention in New Orleans with my family; I didn't know that NDSC convention offered a track of workshops presented in Spanish and another track translated from English to Spanish. I was in my own little world learning everything in English, taking everything in and going back home to share the knowledge with my community; I even bought the recorded audio!

My time at NDSC has taught me so much, from joining NDAC, which is our advocacy group, attending different webinars, using kid's connections at conventions, connecting with minority groups from all over so we can better serve them, and much more. My passion is helping parents, especially our bilingual families; they tend to experience an added layer of isolation. I hope that all parents will know about our organization and learn more about what we do.

Black Down Syndrome Association

The Black Down Syndrome Association is a nonprofit organization dedicated to providing Black families with the resources and support they need for their loved ones with Down Syndrome. Founded in 2022 by two Black mothers who have Black sons with Down syndrome, the organization works to create a culturally competent, safe space for Black families and their loved ones with Down syndrome.

About Black Down Syndrome Association

By Kelli Caughman, Co-Founder of BDSA

In 2015, my world shifted in a way I never expected. Just two weeks before giving birth to my son, I received the news that he would be born with Down syndrome. At that moment, I made a decision. I was not going to hide or whisper about his diagnosis. The day I found out, I told the world. From that moment on, I have been shouting his worth, celebrating every milestone, and standing tall in the truth that my son is extraordinary.

I didn't waver, not even for a moment! I was all in. When I began connecting with the Down syndrome community, I quickly realized that something was missing. Support was readily available, but I longed for connection. A space where I could see and feel my family reflected. At local events and in national groups, I rarely saw other Black families.

That lack of representation stirred something in me. I knew that for many families like mine, belonging mattered as much as support. I volunteered on local and state levels, serving with Down syndrome organizations that gave me valuable experience and relationships. Still, I carried a deep desire to build something that truly reflected our lived experiences as Black parents raising Black children with Down syndrome.

That desire became the foundation of the Black Down Syndrome Association, an organization I co-founded to connect families, celebrate our children, and create a network of support rooted in representation and empowerment. We aim to bridge gaps by providing resources, education, and a strong community where every family feels seen and valued. My hope is that every parent who reads this, no matter where you are on your journey, knows that advocacy begins with love, grows through connection, and thrives in community.

Zoe's Toolbox

Zoe's Toolbox provides boxes of sunshine to families in the first year in the Down syndrome community. These boxes are filled with PT, OT, feeding and speech tools, as well as sensory toys that are greeted toward children six months old to two years of age.

About Zoe's Toolbox

By Karmel Garcia, Founder of Zoe's Toolbox

When we first brought Zoe home, our daughter with Down syndrome, we scheduled her first at home PT session. At the end, the therapist handed me a short list of therapy tools to order that would be helpful to have at home. For some reason, that simple list pushed me to my emotional breaking point. It was just a list of items, but to me it felt like a huge mountain to climb, and the thought of adding anything else to my plate felt impossible. That "mountain" eventually became the inspiration behind our nonprofit Zoe's Toolbox.

Zoe's Toolbox was thoughtfully created with guidance from licensed therapists to include developmental tools to support a child's growth in PT, OT, feeding, speech and sensory input. Our toolboxes are developmental starter kits and are free to all recipients six months to two years of age. A parent, sibling, and loved one are the most important developmental therapy tools a child will ever have, and our hope is that our toolbox and resources empower parents to be their child's greatest advocate.

We are so thankful that Zoe's story is shared with families all across the United States with the beautiful gift of development.

PDS Health Foundation

The Pediatric Dental Service (PDS) Health Foundation has a vision for a world where everyone has a heart for service and a home for oral health so that all people, regardless of where they live, their abilities, or needs can get quality oral health that improves their overall health.

American Academy of Developmental Medicine & Dentistry (AADMD)

The American Academy of Developmental Medicine and Dentistry is a nonprofit, membership organization of interdisciplinary health professionals—including primary care physicians, medical specialists, dentists, nurses, and other clinicians—committed to improving the quality of healthcare for people with intellectual/developmental disabilities (IDD).

About AADMD

By Meelin Dian Chin Kit-Wells, DDS, MEd

President | American Academy of Developmental Medicine & Dentistry (AADMD)
Pediatric Dentist | PDS Health Foundation | Wells Dental, LLC

My name is Dr. Dian, and I am a pediatric dentist who sees children and adults of all ages and abilities. I am inspired every single day. I am honored to provide clinical care at the PDS Health Foundation Special Needs Clinic and doubly honored to serve as president of the American Academy of Developmental Medicine and Dentistry (AADMD), an organization of medical and dental providers dedicated to advocacy, education, and compassionate care for individuals with intellectual and developmental disabilities. I have cherished my years in academia working with dental students and pediatric dental residents, and I recently stepped away from teaching to focus fully on clinical care.

One of my favorite memories from my academic years happened during the winter of 2018, a Buffalo winter, no less. My dental students organized a gingerbread house decorating party at our dental clinic for a group of teenagers and young adults with Down Syndrome. The young adults were excited, but when they arrived, they hesitated at the clinic door. Their parents shared that the hesitation came from fear: they thought they were coming for dental treatment.

(*continued*)

We had to think quickly, so we changed the plan. My students presented our guests with gowns, gloves, and masks and invited our guests to become the dentists for the day. The dental students became their patients. Every guest donned their dental wear and gave their dental student patients rides in the dental chair and instructions on how to brush and floss. Gingerbread houses were eventually decorated, but honestly, no one wanted to stop being a dentist.

When the evening ended, two parents lingered. One shared that her daughter, who had always wanted to be a butterfly, now dreamed of working in dentistry. Another parent, Chris's mom, told us her son's part-time job was coming to an end and she was worried about what came next. She asked, "Would there be a chance for him to work in your office?"

And that moment became the start of our Innovative Internship that I call "Chris Can."

The purpose of the Innovative Internship Program is to give people with disabilities an opportunity to work in a dental office for a set period of time—offering structure, skill-building, confidence, and the possibility of continued employment as part of our team. Chris and his mom completed modified training in infection control, HIPAA, and office protocols. Patients immediately noticed the joy he brought to the clinic. His presence made us better by being more connected, more patient, more human. The dental students loved working with him. And by the end of his internship, thanks to our boss, Chris was officially hired. Today, he is still our "assistant to the assistants," still brightening our days, still reminding us what truly matters.

Families who bring their children to our office often share how comforting it is to see Chris. Our former dental students, dentists now all across the country, still remember that gingerbread house event. I hope they carry forward the lesson: simple acts can open doors that change lives.

I believe we live in a world, and at a moment in time, when this book is very much needed, in much the same way acceptance, encouragement and love is needed.

Whether we are building gingerbread houses, providing person-centered care in the dental chair, or simply reaching out to someone who feels unseen, we each have the ability to break down barriers. We each have the power to say, "You belong here."

And when we do that, when we choose compassion, and connection, well, beautiful things happen.

I think this book will help remind us of that truth.

Other Resources

There are many other resources that can be helpful to you on your journey. I've listed some here:

- **GiGi's Playhouse:** A nonprofit organization that provides free educational, therapeutic, and career development programs for individuals with Down syndrome and their families. It is a network of Down Syndrome Achievement Centers with locations across the United States and Mexico, founded to change how the world views Down syndrome by offering a lifetime of support from birth through career.
- **The National Down Syndrome Society (NDSS):** This is the leading human rights organization for all individuals with Down syndrome. NDSS envisions a world in which all people with Down syndrome have the opportunity to enhance their quality of life, realize their life aspirations and become valued members of welcoming communities. Founded in 1979, NDSS supports and advocates for the Down syndrome community by focusing on three key areas of programming: Resources & Support, Policy & Advocacy and Community Engagement. NDSS engages in various activities and programs that provide support, informational resources, and community engagement opportunities for individuals with Down syndrome and those who support them.
- **Down Syndrome Education International:** This is a leading international research and support organization dedicated to raising levels of educational achievement among children

with Down syndrome. Over the past 40 years, the charity has supported research into the children's specific learning needs and more effective teaching approaches and worked to disseminate evidence-based guidance and practical advice to families and professionals worldwide. By advancing evidence-based practice, Down Syndrome Education International leverages substantial public and nonprofit sector investments in early intervention and education services. Each year, the charity helps over 120,000 families, teachers, therapists, schools, and nonprofit and government service providers in more than 170 countries to provide more effective support to young people with Down syndrome.

- **Jack's Basket:** Jack's Basket is a 501(c)3 nonprofit organization with a mission to celebrate babies with Down syndrome. We strive to ensure that every new and expectant parent is provided resources and avenues of support within the community. We aim to equip medical providers with tools to discuss the diagnosis in an unbiased way in hopes that having a baby with Down syndrome is celebrated like any other. Carissa, the Founder of Jack's Basket, shared her personal story in Chapter 2.
- **RODS Heroes:** The mission of RODS Heroes is to uncover the superpowers of individuals with Down syndrome. This happens through showcasing and celebrating their abilities, inspiring families to answer the call to adopt a child with Down syndrome and empowering communities to support individuals with Down syndrome. Brady Murray, the founder, shares more in the Adoption Chapter.
- **Dear Mom Conference:** Dear Mom, is just that! A dream born from a realization that friendship with another mom raising a person with Down syndrome is one of the strongest tools you'll have on this journey. Dear Mom Conference is needed for us as much as it is needed for you. This is our invitation. That we come to know you, because we are you. You are welcome to join us on this journey, together. To pave new paths for seeking hope, finding your voice, and leaving your fears behind.

- **CaringTide (You heard from the founders, Brady and Jennie, in Chapter 11):** CaringTide provides long-term planning for your whole family, not just the loved one with a disability. CaringTide combines personal experience with professional expertise. Legal Professionals, Certified Financial Planners, Tax Specialists, and Chartered Special Needs Consultants come together to assure your family receives professional guidance and direction that is customized to your unique needs. Our CaringTide team members are passionate advocates for the disability community and bring personal insight and empathy, making our approach both comprehensive and compassionate.
- **Ruby's Rainbow:** Ruby's Rainbow grants scholarships to help students with Down syndrome pursue their higher-education dreams and shows the world about their AMAZING capabilities! Their mission is to support students rockin' that extra chromosome in achieving their dreams of higher education and independence, while spreading awareness of their capabilities and general awesomeness! You read from the Founder, Liz Plachta in Chapter 10.
- **Dads of Down Syndrome:** DODs is for the dads who want to love their families well, learn from others walking the same road, and turn their experience into something that empowers the entire Down syndrome community. They reinvest funds raised back into the community by supporting organizations, initiatives, and families doing meaningful work in the Down syndrome space. Their hope is that more people hear about DODs, so no dad feels like he has to navigate this journey alone, and the communities they serve and support grow stronger.
- **Global Down Syndrome Foundation:** The Global Down Syndrome Foundation is a public nonprofit 501(c)(3) dedicated to significantly improving the lives of people with Down syndrome through Research, Medical Care, Education and Advocacy. Their goal is to significantly improve the lives of people with Down syndrome through Research, Medical Care, Education, and Advocacy. They work to educate governments,

educational organizations, and society in order to affect legislative and social changes so that every person with Down syndrome has an equitable chance at a satisfying life.

- **Down Syndrome Resource Foundation (DSRF):** This is a Canadian-based foundation where the mission is to support people living with Down syndrome and their families with individualized and leading-edge educational programs, health services, information resources, and rich social connections, so each person can flourish in their own right.
- **Rising Kites/Rising Kites Coffee:** The mission of Rising Kites is to celebrate the gift of Down syndrome by bringing encouragement, resources, and support to those within the Down syndrome community. Rising Kites Coffee is a program within Rising Kites, a registered 501(c)3 that: Provides employment and job training opportunities to individuals with intellectual disabilities, fosters an inclusive environment where all individuals are encouraged to see the gift that people with disabilities are to our world, AND helps resources continue to be delivered to the community. Danielle Grandholm, the Founder, shared her personal story in Chapter 3.
- **Hearts of Joy International:** This organization provides lifesaving heart surgery to children all over the world. Their mission is to care for the forgotten, unwanted and vulnerable. They serve children with Down syndrome, particularly in countries where they are stigmatized, abandoned, or denied access to lifesaving heart surgery. In a world that often sees them as less valuable due to poverty, discrimination, or cultural stigma, we affirm their worth as image bearers of God and restore dignity through holistic family-centered care.

CHAPTER 17

Happiness Is. . .

> *"I didn't know what I was supposed to do. . .but I found my way to you."*
>
> —Lyrics to "I Found My Way" by Misty Coy Snyder

"I WISH. . ."

". . .I wish the doctor had called me into the office and not shared the diagnosis over the phone. . ."

". . .I wish the medical professionals had not overloaded me with potential risks and fears at the onset. . ."

". . .I wish everyone at the doctor's office didn't look at me with pity in their eyes. . ."

". . .I wish SOMEONE had said congratulations about my baby instead of treating the diagnosis like a death sentence. . ."

". . .I wish the people around me didn't try to rush me out of my grief. It made me feel a deep sense of shame. . ."

". . .I wish I could have had that gender reveal party but it felt like all the celebration was sucked out of the pregnancy. . ."

It's been established in the pages of this book and within the greater community that, when a family receives a Down syndrome diagnosis, a feeling of loss can ensue. The "I wish" moments and the "What ifs" can dominate the minds of parents and close family and friends, with an accompanying sense of powerlessness. Lack of control. The fantasy in your mind about what your baby would be like can be crushed into a million pieces, and it can take time to put those pieces back together. Eventually, healing can come in the most beautiful and unexpected forms and you realize that the story isn't over. It's just in the process of a rewrite.

And speaking of rewrites, I've thought long and hard about how I WISH my OB had delivered the news to me. This is my personal rewrite:

> OB of my Dreams: "Misty, I would love a moment to chat with you and your husband. Are you able to come into the office today?"
>
> 20 minutes later, my husband and I would be sitting in her office and she would say,
>
> OB of my Dreams: "Thank you for coming in. I wanted to be sure that we had a chance to chat face to face about some results that came back in your NIPT testing. While this can't be 100% confirmed without diagnostic testing, the NIPT came back with a 9/10 chance that your baby will have Down syndrome. I know this is not news you were expecting and might come as a shock or surprise. But I, as your doctor, am here to equip you as best I can, along with the genetic counselor you will see next week. While there are health risks that can sometimes accompany having a child with Down syndrome, there are also very real and beautiful stories that many families have to share about raising their child with Down syndrome. Here are some materials to better inform you about Down syndrome, medically, and here are several flyers to show you the vast array of support that exists for families in your position. You are not alone in this and most importantly, congratulations on your baby boy."

How would *you* rewrite the way you received the news? Maybe you are in a smaller group of families handled with the utmost care and concern.

Either way, we don't get to dictate how the news is delivered to us or those we love. But we CAN dream for better in the future. We can fight to educate, raise awareness, and share our experiences so parents, down the road, receiving the news can stand on solid ground. For those of us who have already walked through those tumultuous diagnosis days and first few years, the greatest rewrite we can achieve is the work we do to change the climate surrounding Down syndrome. The sweetest end to grieving is sharing the joy our precious loved ones bring into our lives. That JOY. That HAPPINESS is what the rest of the world needs shouted from the rooftops. Even still, there will be many who don't understand. The negativity, misinformation and bias abounds, even today. But as we strip away those layers of ableism in our own hearts and minds, we can share our genuine, true, raw, hard, and good and everything in between, stories. This is OUR STORY to tell.

A few years ago, I wrote a song called, "I Found My Way" for Happiness is Down syndrome and a portion of the song says,

3/2/1—right now it sounds so fun.

But it didn't feel that way.

You're the one.

The one that I prayed for, the one that I waited for.

3/2/1—it surely sounds like fun.

And I found my way, I found my way to you.

I didn't know what I was supposed to do.

But I found my way to you.

I didn't know that you could be the one that I longed for.

Who could tell that you would be the one who opened the door?

I wrote this song as a tribute to the Misty of 2020 who just received the news about her son. The difference between how I felt then, sitting in the genetic counselor's office to the present moment, writing this book—for you—is drastically different. It takes my breath away how far my family has come. Slowly, we found our way ***TO*** and ***THROUGH*** Jedidiah. I didn't find answers overnight, and that journey has certainly not been devoid of pain, tears and hardship. But, bit by bit, with the help of the community and organizations shared in this book, I've found my footing, and I ADORE this life with my Jedidiah, "Beloved of God." I know I'm not alone in this sentiment.

One mom in our community describes the arc of this journey very well in "Finding the Magic."

Finding the Magic

By Taylor Koudela, Mom and Advocate in the Down syndrome community

If only 27-year-old me knew what almost 30-year-old me knows now. If only I could have caught a glimpse of this life when I was fearing for my child's life and wondering what would become of mine. . .

When we received our child's prenatal Down syndrome diagnosis, we knew that the trajectory of our life would be forever changed. At the time, we couldn't quite understand the new future we were destined for and to be transparent, we felt a part of us rejecting it. Not rejecting our sweet baby—the love we had for him was deep from the beginning—but rejecting the fears and anxieties, the lifestyle change, the health complications, the inevitable challenges, the unknowns.

As I tried to grapple with this new life, my husband told me something that will be etched on my soul forever—he looked at me, validating the turmoil of emotions I was feeling and said, "There will still be magic," and then it clicked. I began to heal and I morphed into an even better version of myself. Yes, there will be fears and anxieties and challenges and doctor appointments and therapies and medical equipment and whatever else it takes to parent a child with a disability, AND in the midst of it all, there will still be MAGIC. And honestly, I think there's even MORE magic here.

I knew that the extra chromosome would touch and impact every part of Levi, but what I didn't realize was that it would also touch and impact every single part of us as well. The shift in perspective, the deep appreciation, and the fierce love that Down syndrome has given us is truly monumental. We have had the privilege of experiencing firsthand how that extra chromosome can turn the mundane things into magic.

Magic.

Divine.

EXTRA-good.

Happiness.

It's OK if you don't feel all of those adjectives right now. Maybe those words will never resonate with you and, again, that's OK. What's important is that YOU, dear reader, are in the life of someone with Down syndrome who will benefit from your unique characteristics and abilities. I didn't believe that to be true upon receiving my prenatal diagnosis. Quite the opposite. I thought, "I am not the right person for this job! Why not someone else who is more qualified?!" But one evening, I was attending a gala for Hearts of Joy International, here in New Jersey. The Founder, Lauren Costabile, shared her story at the podium and pointed out her single palmar crease on her palm (which is most commonly attributed to individuals with Down syndrome), sharing that God's plan was literally written on her palm. I casually glanced down at my palms and saw, for the first time, that my left palm ALSO had a single palmar crease. Tears filled my eyes because I once thought I was so, very unqualified for this job as Jed's mom. And yet, there I sat, with a clear marker for this path I was walking. A path that is surely not easy. But GOOD.

While most people look at Down syndrome through the lens of deficit, I'm here to testify that my son has ABUNDANCE. He doesn't just have an extra chromosome, he has an abundance of empathy, intuition, compassion, and love. To those who've never been close to someone with Down syndrome, all of this might sound like an exaggeration. A consolation prize. But anyone who has encountered an individual with an extra chromosome knows exactly what I'm talking about—an undeniable abundance.

I began this book with a story about my acting days in New York City. There, in the prime of my life, sitting on top of the world in many ways, I encountered a group of individuals with disabilities and one man, with Down syndrome. His mere presence made me uncomfortable and I just didn't have the time to listen, learn, and observe a neurodivergent individual. I had things to do, places to see, songs to sing, happiness and contentment to find! The encounter was an unwanted diversion from my main goal. I didn't have words for it then, but I can now identify my reaction as fear and ignorance. I didn't know what I didn't know. Leading up to that moment with the starry-eyed tourist, I'd never had a chance to know and love someone with Down syndrome.

Eleven years later, on a cold evening in November, I drove my two sons to the park with tears in my eyes. The stress and overwhelm of my schedule had gotten the better of me, and I had to breathe deeply and refocus. In the dim light, two sets of eyes peered at me through the rearview mirror and, despite my efforts to hide the tears, they clearly saw I was in distress. When we arrived, my older son unbuckled himself and ran to his favorite slide. I lifted Jed out of his car seat and fully expected him to run to his brother's side. Instead, he stepped right in front of me and looked up at me with warmth in his eyes. He moved his finger from his eye down his cheek (the sign for "sad") and he said, "Mom—are hu ohay?" I smiled through my tears and said, "yes baby—mommy will be okay." He lifted his arms up and I picked him up. He wrapped his arms around me and began to pat my shoulder while saying, "Are hu ohay? Ohay, mom?"

When I tell you that I have never felt so seen in my entire life, I'm not exaggerating. He filled a spot in my heart that was aching.

This is the extra.

This is the abundance.

This is Down syndrome.

Happiness **IS** Down syndrome.

Resources

The following are the resources featured in this book, along with the websites of many contributors in this book, alphabetized by name. Reach out to any and all!

Adult Down Syndrome Center: https://adscresources.advocatehealth.com/about/

American Academy of Developmental Medicine and Dentistry: https://www.aadmd.org

Amy Julia Becker, Mother in the Down Syndrome Community, MDiv, Advocate, Author, Podcaster: http://amyjuliabecker.com

Angela O'Brien, Mother in the Down Syndrome Community, Advocate, Professional Organizer, Podcaster: https://yourspacereclaimed.net/

Audrey Presby and Jeremy Fraser, Self Advocates, Podcasters: https://www.youtube.com/channel/UCpdjR2c5pAXgnVYzluVHnQA

Black Down Syndrome Association (BDSA): https://www.blackdownsyndrome.org

Brian Skotko, Director of the Down Syndrome Program at Massachusetts General Hospital: https://brianskotko.com/

Cami Nelson, Photographer in the Disability Community: https://www.camilynnephotography.com/

CaringTide: https://caringtide.com/

Carolina Elias, Sister in the Down Syndrome Community, Producer and Advocate: https://carolinaelias.com/

Dads of Down Syndrome: https://dadsofdownsyndrome.org

Dashiell Meyer, Self-Advocate, Speaker, Filmmaker, Actor, Athlete: https://dashiellmeier.com/

Dear Mom, Conference: https://www.dearmomco.com

Down Syndrome Diagnosis Network (DSDN): https://www.dsdiagnosisnetwork.org

Down Syndrome Education (DSE): https://www.down-syndrome.org/en-us/

Down Syndrome Resource Foundation: https://dsrf.org/

Elizabeth Wofford, Mother in the Down Syndrome Community, PhD and LPC/S: https://swallowsnestcc.com

Extra Community on Facebook: https://www.facebook.com/share/g/1888s4ztEx/?mibextid=wwXIfr

GiGi's Playhouse: https://gigisplayhouse.org/

Global Down Syndrome Foundation: https://www.globaldownsyndrome.org/

Happiness is Down syndrome on Facebook: https://www.facebook.com/p/Happiness-is-Down-Syndrome-100068296297329/

Happiness is Down syndrome on Instagram: https://www.instagram.com/happinessisdownsyndrome/?hl=en

Hearts of Joy International: https://heartsofjoyinternational.com/

Heather Avis, Mother in the Down Syndrome Community, NY Times Best Selling Author, Advocate, Speaker, Podcaster: http://heatheravis.com

Heather Vukelich, M.S. CCC-SLP: https://happykidstherapy.com/

Holly Simon, Mother in the Down Syndrome Community, Advocate, Author, Public Speaker: https://21pineapples.com

Jack's Basket: https://jacksbasket.org/

Jackson and David Hughens, Father/Son Filmmaking Duo: https://madewithlovethemovie.com/

Jill Rabin, M.S. CCC-SLP/L IBCLC: https://jillrabin.com/

Kimberly Yaeger, Founder and President of Little Leaf Learning Center Inc: https://mylittleleaf.org/about/

Manni Coe, Brother in the Down Syndrome Community, Sunday Times Bestselling Author and Advocate: https://mannicoe.com/

Matthew Schwab, Self-Advocate, Public Speaker, Advocate: https://matthewschwabspeaks.com/

Mia Rodriguez, Self-Advocate, Singer, Speaker: https://mianoellerodriguez.com/

National Down Syndrome Congress: https://www.ndsccenter.org

National Down Syndrome Society (NDSS): https://ndss.org/

PDS Health Foundation, Special Needs Dentistry: https://www.pdsfoundation.org/programs/special-needs/

Rising Kites: https://www.risingkites.org/

RODS Heroes: https://www.rods.org

Ruby's Rainbow: https://rubysrainbow.org/

Simone's Oasis: https://simones-oasis.org/

Sofia Sanchez, Self-Advocate, Speaker, Actress, Model: https://www.sofia-sanchez.com/

Team Iron Will: https://teamironwill.org

Tonye Faloughi-Ekezie, Mother in the Down Syndrome Community, Advocate and Founder of Simone's Oasis: https://simones-oasis.org/

Virginia Wear, Mother in the Down Syndrome Community, Advocate, Author, Speaker, Podcaster: https://podcasts.apple.com/us/podcast/the-formed-life-podcast/id1826482126

Zoe's Toolbox: https://www.zoes-toolbox.com/

Notes

Introduction

1. Stotko, B. @brianskotko. July 27, 2026. Better information thanks to research [Video]. Instagram. https://www.instagram.com/brianskotko/.

Chapter 2

1. Chicoine, B. January 2025. Life Expectancy, Aging, and the Down Syndrome Population, Advocate Medical Group. https://adscresources.advocatehealth.com/resources/aging-and-life-expectancy/#:~:text=By%201984%2C%20the%20life%20expectancy,general%20health%20management%20(1).

Chapter 3

1. Piaget, J. (1952). The origins of intelligence in children. International Universities Press.
2. Bowlby, J. (1969). Attachment and loss: Vol. 1. Attachment. Basic Books.
3. Bowlby, J. (1980). Attachment and loss: Vol. 3. Loss. Basic Books.
4. Harris, D. L., & Winokuer, H. R. (2019). Principles and practice of grief counseling. Springer Publishing Company.
5. Briere, J., & Scott, C. (2025). Principles of trauma therapy: A guide to symptoms, evaluation, and treatment (3rd ed.). Sage.
6. Boelen, P. A., & van den Bout, J. (2005). Complicated grief, depression, and anxiety as distinct postloss syndromes: A confirmatory factor analysis study. American Journal of Psychiatry, 162(11), 2175–2177. https://doi.org/10.1176/appi.ajp.162.11.2175.

7. Shear, M. K. (2015). Complicated grief. New England Journal of Medicine, 372(2), 153–160. https://doi.org/10.1056/NEJMcp1315618.
8. Stroebe, M., Schut, H., & Stroebe, W. (2007). Health outcomes of bereavement. The Lancet, 370(9603), 1960–1973. https://doi.org/10.1016/S0140-6736(07)61816-9.
9. Buckley, T., Sunari, D., Marshall, A., Bartrop, R., McKinley, S., & Tofler, G. (2012). Physiological correlates of bereavement and the impact of bereavement interventions. Progress in Cardiovascular Diseases, 55(2), 99–106. https://doi.org/10.1016/j.pcad.2012.07.004.
10. Lannen, P. K., Wolfe, J., Prigerson, H. G., Onelov, E., & Kreicbergs, U. C. (2008). Unresolved grief in a national sample of bereaved parents: Impaired mental and physical health 4 to 9 years later. Journal of Clinical Oncology, 26(36), 5870–5876. https://doi.org/10.1200/JCO.2007.14.6738.
11. Stroebe, M., Schut, H., & Stroebe, W. (2007). Health outcomes of bereavement. The Lancet, 370(9603), 1960–1973. https://doi.org/10.1016/S0140-6736(07)61816-9.
12. Burke, L. A., Neimeyer, R. A., & McDevitt-Murphy, M. E. (2010). African American homicide bereavement: Aspects of social support that predict complicated grief, PTSD, and depression. Omega: Journal of Death and Dying, 61(1), 1–24. https://doi.org/10.2190/OM.61.1.a.
13. Neimeyer, R. A., Klass, D., & Dennis, M. R. (2014). A social constructionist account of grief: Meaning making as the central process in grief. Death Studies, 38(6–10), 485–498. https://doi.org/10.1080/07481187.2014.913454.
14. Stroebe, W., Stroebe, M., & Schut, H. (2001). Gender differences in adjustment to bereavement: An empirical and theoretical review. Review of General Psychology, 5(1), 62–83. https://doi.org/10.1037/1089-2680.5.1.62.
15. Burke, L. A., & Neimeyer, R. A. (2014). Spiritual distress in bereavement: Evolution of a research program. Religions, 5(4), 1087–1115. https://doi.org/10.3390/rel5041087.
16. Neimeyer, R. A. (2001). Meaning reconstruction & the experience of loss. American Psychological Association.

17. Wortmann, J. H., & Park, C. L. (2009). Religion/spirituality and change in meaning after bereavement: Qualitative evidence for the meaning making model. Journal of Loss and Trauma, 14(1), 17–34. https://doi.org/10.1080/15325020802173876.
18. Corden, A., Hirst, M., & Nice, K. (2010). Financial implications of death of a partner. Bereavement Care, 29(3), 30–34. https://doi.org/10.1080/02682621.2010.522373.
19. Hansson, R. O., & Stroebe, M. S. (Eds.). (2007). Bereavement in late life: Coping, attachment, and developmental influences. American Psychological Association.
20. Aoun, S. M., Breen, L. J., Howting, D. A., Rumbold, B., McNamara, B., & Hegney, D. (2014). Who needs bereavement support? A population-based survey of bereavement risk and support need. PLOS ONE, 9(3), e90508. https://doi.org/10.1371/journal.pone.0090508.
21. Eisma, M. C. (2023). Prolonged grief disorder in ICD-11 and DSM-5-TR: Challenges and controversies. Australian & New Zealand Journal of Psychiatry, 57(7), 944–951.
22. Prigerson, H. G., Horowitz, M. J., Jacobs, S. C., Parkes, C. M., Aslan, M., Goodkin, K., & Maciejewski, P. K. (2009). Prolonged grief disorder: Psychometric validation of criteria proposed for DSM-V and ICD-11. PLOS Medicine, 6(8), e1000121. https://doi.org/10.1371/journal.pmed.1000121.
23. Schulz, R., Boerner, K., Shear, K., Zhang, S., & Gitlin, L. N. (2006). Predictors of complicated grief among dementia caregivers: A prospective study of bereavement. American Journal of Geriatric Psychiatry, 14(8), 650–658. https://doi.org/10.1097/01.JGP.0000191328.48576.04.
24. Song, Y. (2023). NIPT test results: Normal range/low risk. https://3billion.io/blog/nipt-test-results-normal-range-low-risk.

Chapter 4

1. Fergus, K. Down Syndrome: Symptoms and Intellectual and Physical Traits. Verywell Health, October 23, 2025. https://www.verywellhealth.com/symptoms-of-down-syndrome-1120463#:~:text=People%20with%20Down%20syndrome%20sometimes,%2C%20dressing%2C%20and%20toilet%20training.

2. Gómez, R. L., & Edgin, J. O. (June 20, 2015). Sleep as a window into early neural development: Shifts in sleep-dependent learning effects across early childhood. Child Development Perspectives, 9(3), 183–189. https://doi.org/10.1111/cdep.12130.
3. Downs Syndrome Association. Sleep - Downs Syndrome Association. April 11, 2025. https://www.downs-syndrome.org.uk/about-downs-syndrome/health-and-wellbeing/sleep/#:~:text=This%20is%20where%20a%20person's,likelihood%20of%20behavioural%20sleep%20problems.
4. Massachusetts Down Syndrome Congress. Preparing to Breastfeed Your Baby With Down Syndrome: A Prenatal Guide - MDSC. MDSC, September 2, 2025. https://mdsc.org/resource/preparing-to-breastfeed-your-baby-with-down-syndrome-a-prenatal-guide/.
5. Massachusetts Down Syndrome Congress. Preparing to Breastfeed Your Baby With Down Syndrome: A Guide for the First Few Hours - MDSC. MDSC, September 2, 2025. https://mdsc.org/resource/preparing-to-breastfeed-your-baby-with-down-syndrome-a-guide-for-the-first-few-hours/.
6. Down Syndrome Pregnancy 2026. Breastfeeding and Down Syndrome | Down Syndrome Pregnancy, n.d. https://downsyndromepregnancy.org/book/breastfeeding-and-down-syndrome/.

Chapter 6

1. Vanderbilt University. "Divorce Rates Lower Among Parents of Children With Down Syndrome," January 8, 2008. https://news.vanderbilt.edu/2008/01/08/divorce-rates-lower-among-parents-of-children-with-down-syndrome-56798/#:~:text=D.%2C%20and%20Robert%20Hodapp%2C,with%20other%20congenital%20birth%20defects.
2. National Down Syndrome Society (NDSS). "Facts, Myths, & Truths About Down Syndrome," n.d. https://ndss.org/myths-truths#myth-down-syndrome-is-a-rare-disorder.

Chapter 7

1. Skotko, B. G., Levine, S. P., & Goldstein, R. (September 9, 2011). Having a brother or sister with Down syndrome: Perspectives from siblings. American Journal of Medical Genetics Part A, 155 (10), 2348–2359. https://doi.org/10.1002/ajmg.a.34228.
2. Clinic, Cleveland. (June 30, 2025). Always Coping, Rarely Seen: Explaining Glass Child Syndrome. Cleveland Clinic, https://health.clevelandclinic.org/glass-child.
3. Stotko, B. @brianskotko. September 11, 2026. Sibling relationships [Video]. Instagram. https://www.instagram.com/brianskotko/.

Chapter 9

1. Buckley, S., Bird, G., Sacks, B., & Archer, T. (January 1, 2006). A comparison of mainstream and special education for teenagers with down syndrome: Implications for parents and teachers. Down Syndrome Research and Practice, 9(3), 54–67. https://doi.org/10.3104/reports.295.

Chapter 10

1. Nleavitt, & Nleavitt. "Understanding Ableism: How Language Shapes Inclusion." Northeast Arc, March 5, 2025. https://ne-arc.org/2025/03/05/understanding-ableism-how-language-shapes-inclusion/#:~:text=What%20is%20Ableism?,that%20reinforce%20stereotypes%20about%20disability.
2. Sense. "What Is Ableism?—Sense," May 31, 2024. https://www.sense.org.uk/information-and-advice/life-stages/ableism-and-disablism/#:~:text=The%20following%20are%20some%20common%20ableism%20examples:,they%20%E2%80%9Cdon't%20look%20disabled%E2%80%9D%20as%20a%20compliment.

Chapter 12

1. Temp, M., & Price, J. (January 9, 2020). How to Build Support System for Adult Children With Disabilities. San Diego Union-Tribune, https://www.sandiegouniontribune.com/2020/01/09/how-to-build-support-system-for-adult-children-with-disabilities/.

Chapter 14

1. TEDx Talks. "The Power of Bravery | Sofia Sanchez | TEDxReno," May 6, 2024. https://www.youtube.com/watch?v=qJTJ9t4IAs8.

Acknowledgments

Special thanks to the team at Wiley Publishing, Jossey Bass; specifically, Sam Ofman for approaching me with the idea for this book and for trusting me to put pen to paper.

To Brady Murray, a friend and mentor who wrote the foreword to this book and created two organizations I am passionate about, RODS Heroes and CaringTide.

To Tiffany Fuller who provided her original and beautiful Karyotype artwork, along with the SMART chart she created.

To Robert Tichio, my brother and friend, who has practiced generosity in every form when it comes to this book and so many ventures of mine.

To Kaitlin Jones who allowed me to interview her, in person, when she was very pregnant with her precious daughter with Down syndrome.

To all the members of the Down syndrome community who have contributed to this book in a variety of ways. Thank you to the organizations, self-advocates, scientists, doctors, specialists, educators in this book and beyond who have worked tirelessly to provide resources, personal testimonies, support, and encouragement to families like mine.

To my family by blood (particularly my parents who have encouraged my writing since I was young), my mentor Dorothy, my wonderful Renaissance Church Family, and my friends and followers, near and far who have supported these life transitions of mine from performer, to mom, to advocate, to writer, to speaker, to Creative Director and WHO KNOWS what else!

To Jesus, who is my reason for living. He's given me life, breath, heart, blessing upon blessing, and lesson after lesson.

My most heartfelt thanks goes to Braden and Clay. Thank you for making adjustments as I left to go to Starbucks to write this book every evening, for months at a time. Thank you for loving me. For making me laugh. For inspiring me. For lifting me up.

. . . and Jed—I owe this all to you, my love. You have introduced me to the Happiness of . . . YOU.

About the Author

For more than 20 years, Misty Coy Snyder has been inspiring people through storytelling. Whether she is onstage taking the audience on a journey through her acting, transporting people through her vocal performance, or challenging and edifying her readers through her writing, Misty relishes connection, and community.

She utilizes her gifts as a performer, entrepreneur, and content creator to advocate for and lift up the disability community. Upon receiving a Down syndrome diagnosis for her second son, Jed, she created a worldwide platform to promote inclusion and awareness called Happiness is Down Syndrome.

Shortly thereafter she launched a podcast called *Bold Voices, Soft Hearts*, featuring stories of those who have discovered their passion through pain. Misty was honored to speak on a panel at the United Nations discussing community support for the Down syndrome community and she travels globally sharing her story of hope.

Misty LOVES connecting through her platforms, @mistycoysnyder and @happinessisdownsyndrome on social media and through her website, mistycoysnyder.com. Reach out and say hello!

Index